Love Knows No

An inspirational study of
The Book of Ruth

Margaret Hess

This book is designed for your personal reading pleasure and profit. It is also designed for group study. A Leader's Guide with helps and hints for teachers and with visual aids (Victor Multiuse Transparency Masters) is available from your local bookstore or from the publisher at $2.25.

VICTOR BOOKS
a division of SP Publications, Inc., Wheaton, Illinois
Offices also in Fullerton, California • Whitby, Ontario, Canada • London, England

Unless otherwise noted, all Scripture quotations are taken from the King James Version. Other versions used are the *New American Standard Version* (NASB) © 1960, 1962, 1963, 1968, 1971, 1972, 1973, the Lockman Foundation, La Habra, California; *The New Scofield Reference Bible* (SCO.) © 1967 by the delegates of the Oxford University Press, Inc., New York; the *Revised Standard Version* (RSV) © 1946, 1952 by the Division of Christian Education of the National Council of the Churches of Christ in the United States of America; the *Amplified Bible* (AMP) © 1965 Zondervan Publishing House, Grand Rapids, Michigan.

Recommended Dewey Decimal Classification: 222.35
        or 920.72
Suggested subject heading: RUTH

Library of Congress Catalog Card Number: 78-64506
ISBN: 0-88207-780-5

VICTOR BOOKS
A division of SP Publications, Inc.
P.O. Box 1825 • Wheaton, Illinois 60187

Contents

Introduction

You find yourself caught in a spider's web of relationships—some good, some bad. You want to relate lovingly with your parents, with your children, with your husband or wife. You must relate to co-workers, boss, or employees. You try to relate to neighbors, to relatives, to strangers. You want to improve your relationship with God. How do you manage all this? The Book of Ruth can tell you how.

In this little book of less than 100 verses, God teaches us in story form. In other parts of the Bible He instructs by direct commandments, by miracles, by prophecies, by wise proverbs and by great events. In Ruth's story, through simple pictures of domestic life, we see what works, and what doesn't work, in human relationships. As we look deeply, we discover that our faith most truly expresses itself in relationships.

The story of Ruth illustrates love's power to surmount all barriers. Here we find one of the most beautiful avowals of love in all literature. Curiously, it expresses the devotion of a young widow for her mother-in-law who has learned to love two pagan daughters-in-law. Both daughters-in-law respond in kind to her love. One, Ruth, climbs over cultural and religious barriers to love her mother-in-law's God.

We see the power of love conquering all natural hostilities. A wealthy landowner shows care to his workmen. He demonstrates love to the poor who want some benefit from him. We see love subduing all prejudice. This wealthy landowner provides for and finally marries a foreigner. To him, Ruth's love for God outweighs her ancestry.

The Book of Ruth displays one picture after another of outstanding personal relationships. Beyond the pictures, we see God's hand showing us how we can beautify our relationships.

We watch life in all its passages, moods, passions, and wishes. Events in Ruth touch the common experiences of all humanity. We identify with Naomi, the bereaved mother-in-law who finds new joy. We live through the experiences of Ruth, the young widow who finds new life and love. We identify with Boaz, a man who manages his love life and business life well.

In the Book of Ruth we sense the presence of God in human relationships, making them His means of grace for our daily lives.

1

When Do You Move?

A high school principal, father of three small children, fell in love with a beautiful redhead, one of his students. He wanted to marry her, but didn't believe in divorce. He and the girl plotted to have his wife killed. He paid someone $2,000 to do the job. He felt cheated when that person pocketed the money without accomplishing the assigned murder.

By juggling funds, the assistant manager of a branch bank embezzled enough money to set up her boyfriend in business. She also bought him a Mercedes. She felt justified in her actions; after all, her bank and others had refused him a loan.

In a power blackout in New York City, a girl asked several boys to help her carry away some loot from a store. Instead, they carried off the loot for themselves. She complained that what they did wasn't right. She didn't see anything wrong with her own actions—she was only seeking to improve her condition of life.

7

"In the days when the judges ruled . . ." (1:1)

What do all these people hold in common? Each believed what he was doing was right. That is how people lived in the days when the judges ruled. No king set standards or restrained their actions. "In those days there was no king in Israel; every man did that which was right in his own eyes" (Jud. 21:25).

In its beginnings, the nation of Israel was a theocracy. God had given the Law through Moses. He had set up a priesthood to teach it. He had set up a system of worship to stamp it on people's minds.

Many people then as now didn't want to confine themselves to following God's direction. Behind the action in Judges, we hear the clash of arms. On the center of the stage, we see horrible murders. We read about intrigues to kill and destroy. We shudder at cruelty, lust, greed, and gross immorality.

Backstage, however, the Director is preparing for a later act. Three people who love God are living out their own quiet lives, uninfluenced by the conditions around them. God is preparing Ruth and Naomi and Boaz for their time on center stage, when they will create a special kind of home life. That family life will later produce David and the kings of Judah, and ultimately Christ. Such people inspire us not to use conditions in and around us as excuses for sin or mediocrity.

In the Book of Ruth we see God's concern with the intimate affairs of human life. We learn that not all history is written in mighty deeds of war and state. Each of us has something to say to our own age which no other person can say. Our lives and our relationships matter.

". . . There was a famine in the land" (1:1).

God has in the past communicated with people through famine or want. The Bible says He speaks to us through rain, sunshine, good crops, bounteous harvests. He also speaks to us through hardship. In the Bible, famine speaks of testing or judgment, and of God's desire to bring us close to Himself.

He tested Abraham with famine in the land, so the patriarch went to Egypt seeking bread (Gen. 12:10). When Isaac was tested with a famine, he simply dug more wells and stayed.

God used famine to send the family of Jacob down to Egypt under Joseph. There they grew into a nation. God led that nation out of Egypt into a land flowing with milk and honey. But He warned that disobedience would bring famine and other disasters. "I will make your heaven as iron" (Lev. 26:19).

The young man in Luke 15 grew bored with conditions of plenty in the place where he grew up. So he asked for his share of the inheritance, and went off to live without restraint. When a famine came and he was hungry, he came to himself, remembering that even hired servants on his father's estate had enough to eat. Then he returned to where he should have stayed in the first place.

In the time of Elimelech and Naomi, God was trying to talk to people through famine. They needed to get back to Him, but they didn't listen. Elimelech and Naomi loved God and meant to serve Him, but they had to earn a living. You can't neglect your family. You have to go where the job is.

"A certain man of Bethlehem-Judah went to sojourn in the country of Moab, he, and his wife, and his two sons" (1:1).

For Elimelech and Naomi, famine came in the most unlikely of all places—Bethlehem. The name means "House of Bread." Bethlehem's old place name was "Ephrah"—Place of Fruit. Its modern name is Beit-lahm, or Flesh-house. No one expected famine there.

The flatroofed houses of Bethlehem occupied a wide ridge above a rich valley. From Bethlehem people could look down to the fields of grain moving with the wind.

Between the town and the fertile fields far below, grape vines grew. Also, fig and olive trees flourished on the terraced slopes. Famine had to be severe to affect Bethlehem.

Today you can visit these fields of Boaz. They're the same fields where the youthful David was trained in the household of Jesse. They're also the fields where angels announced the birth of Christ in Bethlehem, some 11 centuries after Elimelech.

The thing that no one thought could happen did happen. Elimelech, who farmed the fields his ancestors had tilled, felt the pinch. People of the town cast about for what to do. Most decided to stick it out.

After a recent drought in California. the whole country feared California's crops would be wiped out. But their crops—pecans, plums, oranges, rice, lettuce—turned out close to normal. With irrigation water reduced or cut off, farmers sank new wells. They opened up old ones. They put in new systems that used water more economically. And they got by.

Most people in Bethlehem survived somehow. They were still there more than 10 years later when Naomi came back. Boaz obviously was thriving.

Elimelech and Naomi decided to go to Moab— just temporarily, of course. They planned only to sojourn—literally, "live as strangers"—in Moab. They felt quite sure they could keep themselves separate from pagan society around them.

But Moab—of all places! The Moabites were longtime enemies of the people of God. They had done their best to prevent the Israelites from approaching the land under Moses (Num. 25:1-3).

Moabites worshiped their cruel god, Chemosh, in such horrible ways. Their fertility rites amounted to sex orgies. These certainly constituted a temptation to the young men of Israel. And Elimelech and Naomi had two young sons growing up. The Moabites also sought to keep evil away with human sacrifice. They sought to bring good luck by sacrificing their own children to their gods.

Elimelech and Naomi sold off some of the sheep they owned, perhaps took a few with them. They packed up their belongings into bags slung over the backs of donkeys. They shut up their little house built of the local limestone. They started out to travel the six miles north to Jerusalem along the ridge of mountains. From Jerusalem they would descend through the hilly wilderness of Judea to the Jordan River. Today you can make the trip from Jerusalem to the Jordan in an hour. Then, on foot and by donkey, it would occupy at least a day.

Once at the Jordan they'd need to get to one of the places for fording the muddy river. They'd wade through foot-deep water, then climb up the hills toward the rolling plateau of Moab's rich pasture lands. The total journey would amount to about 50 miles, two or three days of travel.

Should they have gone to Moab? Some say no. They were already in the place of God's appointment in Bethlehem. Others say yes. If they hadn't gone to Moab, Ruth would never had come to know God. What do you say?

God rules and overrules. Perhaps on the face of it they did make a mistake in going to Moab. Yet we see how God can use our mistakes for His glory when we truly want to serve Him.

"And the name of the man was Elimelech and the name of his wife Naomi, and the name of his two sons Mahlon and Chilion, Ephrathites of Bethlehem-judah. And they came into the country of Moab, and continued there" (1:2).

Unfortunately, makeshift arrangements all too often become permanent. You wear a dress you made without quite completing some inside seams. You think you'll finish them a little later. You may never get those seams bound.

You start dating a boy or girl without thinking whether he or she would really make a good marriage partner. You drift into marriage. The temporary becomes permanent.

You take a certain job because it's the one most readily available. Perhaps it pays the most at the time. You spend your whole life in a field of work you didn't really choose.

Elimelech, whose name means "my God is King," left the land of promise to live temporarily in pagan Moab. He settled down and stayed.

America is called a nation of nomads. Twenty percent of Americans move every year. The average person moves 14 times in his lifetime. What reasons propel us into such motion?

1. People move from necessity. Throughout history, some have become refugees by compulsion. The Jews scattered throughout the nations have often been driven from place to place by forces beyond themselves. During World War II, Hitler drove Jews out of Germany, their centuries-long homeland. In the 18th century, the Catholic majority drove a Protestant minority, the Huguenots, out of France.

2. Economic situations impel people to move. Ireland's potato famine of 1848 brought many Irish to America, including the Kennedy family. Today, a business may move to another city. A person may move with the company rather than lose his job. Sometimes a whole industry dries up. A person must find another job. If he can't find one locally, he must search elsewhere, and go where the job is.

3. Sometimes, people must move for their health. The son of a young minister in Indiana suffered from severe asthma. Doctors told the parents only a dry climate would help him. The family moved to the Southwest. The father served various churches in southwestern states for the rest of his ministry. The five children went to school and grew up there. All settled in Arizona or California.

4. At times, people move to run away from something. They don't like their neighbors, or they're tired of shoveling snow. Maybe they want to escape

from interfering in-laws. They cross a continent to find independence. Sometimes these moves turn out well, sometimes not.

A young couple tried in every way to tell the girl's mother to let them live their own lives. They wanted the privilege of learning from their own mistakes. The mother telephoned or stopped in every day. She checked on the dusting, scrutinized the contents of the refrigerator, and rearranged the furniture. She wanted to be consulted about every purchase. She pitched in and "helped" when no one asked for help, carried the laundry home, and took over the cooking whenever she came. The girl wanted a chance to grow up. The young couple moved to California to escape her.

An older couple sold their home of many years, packed up their furniture, and bought a home in Florida. They bid good-bye to their church and friends. A year later they came back to visit their former haunts. They hadn't found a church they liked, and they missed their old friends. They wished for their old home. But somebody else lived in it now.

5. Often people move to better themselves. A rising young executive must move to climb the corporation ladder. His superiors want him to gain experience in all aspects of the company's work. It may mean a move every year or two for the family.

A young man in his early thirties moved to another city to join a new company. He knew the level he wanted to reach by the age of 35, and saw that these promotions would not come where he worked.

Sometimes families move for the sake of offering a better education to their children.

6. Some people move simply for adventure. A successful architect always wanted to live in the Pacific Northwest. He gave up his fine position, found another one similar to it in Seattle, and moved his reluctant family from a suburb of Chicago to the Seattle area.

7. People move to rejoin family and friends. A couple originally from Atlanta, Georgia, spent most of their working lives in Bloomfield Hills, Michigan. Everyone assumed they considered it their home. But when they retired they moved back to Atlanta.

8. Sometimes people move because they feel a call of God to live in a certain place. God told Abraham, "Get thee out of thy country, and from thy kindred, and from thy father's house, unto a land that I will show thee . . . and I will bless thee, . . . and thou shalt be a blessing" (Gen. 12:1-2).

The assistant to the president of Detroit Edison Company moved from a luxurious suburb of Detroit to a racially mixed neighborhood in the city. He bought an attractive home and sank his roots to work in his church there. He felt called of God to live and minister in that community.

Later, he had opportunities to go abroad on a "lend-lease" basis under the United States government. While still employed by Detroit Edison, he spent a year in Taiwan helping them improve their electrical systems. On his own time, he worked in a volunteer capacity alongside missionaries.

He spent another year in the city of Teheran. There he taught a Sunday School class of Americans, helping them see how they could witness for Christ in Iran.

The same man accepted an opportunity to spend

three years in Saudi Arabia as an electrical consultant. While there, he gathered Americans together, he conducted services, and helped them form a church.

A high school English teacher searched about for a place to retire. She settled on Cicero, Illinois, then a Czech community, and bought a modest home. She joined a church, and was able to teach and minister in many ways in the church and community. Why? Because she spoke Czechoslovakian fluently, and wanted to witness for Jesus Christ among Czech people.

A friend of mine, who has moved 17 times in 18 years of marriage, wrote me a note just before her last move. "Your [Bible] class . . . has brought such joy to me during my brief stay in Birmingham . . . It is difficult to keep life in the right perspective when so much happens to continuously uproot a person, but your class has helped me to keep everything in focus. You've helped me to see how I can be secure at all times in serving the Lord wherever I am . . . Affectionately, Elizabeth."

I live in a suburb of Detroit. An article, rating the desirability of cities as places to live, ranks Detroit as 48th among 50. Yet I feel very happy. Why? My husband accepted a call to a church here. We felt very sure God wanted us to serve that church.

In the first church we served, we wanted terribly to move. We stayed there for seven long years. The neighborhood was difficult, the church slow to respond. We didn't realize we needed to learn some very important lessons. The Lord showed us it was time to move only when we had learned those lessons.

When do you move? Sometimes you have no choice. Sometimes you search the Scriptures to look for parallels to your situation. Joseph was packed off to Egypt when his brothers sold him to slave merchants (Gen. 37:28-36). Paul traveled to spread the Gospel.

You look for principles to show you if this is God's move for you. You pray about the move. You may put out a fleece, as did Gideon (Jud. 6:36-40). You ask God to show you through circumstances. "And thine ears shall hear a word behind thee, saying, 'This is the way, walk ye in it' " (Isa. 30:21).

"And Elimelech, Naomi's husband died; and she was left, and her two sons" (1:3).

Elimelech and Naomi left Bethlehem during a time of distress to avoid participating in it. In Moab they experienced far worse difficulties. First, Elimelech died. At this point Naomi might have decided to go back to Bethlehem, as a widow with two sons. But she stayed on in Moab.

We wonder what Naomi's responsibility was in the move. Was she an active or a passive person? Maybe she put the idea of going to Moab into Elimelech's mind in the first place. Or maybe she went along only as an obedient wife. At any rate, she didn't go back to Bethlehem as soon as Elimelech died.

"And they took them wives of the women of Moab; and the name of the one was Orpah, and the name of the other Ruth; and they dwelled there about ten years" (1:4).

As Naomi stayed on in Moab, her two sons married Moabite girls. Not too surprising. They reached marriageable age, and Moabite girls were the only ones around. They settled down, literally the word means "sat there," about 10 years.

"And Mahlon and Chilion died also both of them; and the woman was left of her two sons and her husband" (1:5).

The names of the two sons mean "sickness" and "wasting." Even back in the Land of Promise the family line was apparently growing weaker. Here in Moab they died. Was God speaking more and more loudly to Naomi through circumstances? We don't know. The text in Ruth utters no condemnation of either Elimelech or Naomi for their move. Certainly they didn't escape suffering by running away from difficulty.

2

Have You Found Rest?

———— ● ————

Three characters have been subtracted in our drama, and two added—all in the first five verses. A husband and two sons have died. Naomi has emerged as the dominant character, with two foreign daughters-in-law. What could anybody make out of that relationship?

"Then she arose with her daughters-in-law, that she might return from the country of Moab . . ." (1:6).

These words are like peepholes through a solid board fence on a construction site, marked "for sidewalk superintendents." We all like to stop and peer through such holes to see what's going on. Here we can look at the home life of Naomi and her two daughters-in-law. How did Naomi create such a beautiful relationship with two foreign daughters-in-law? Imagine either of them considering going back with her to her own country!

Imagine how Naomi must have felt when her two sons chose Moabite women to marry. She certainly knew of the regulations laid down in the Law of Moses. The Law said a Moabite couldn't enter into the congregation of the Lord even to the tenth generation (Deut. 23:3). God had specifically warned against intermarriage with foreign nations. He feared they would turn away His people from serving Him (Deut. 7:3-4).

Many children marry someone their parents wouldn't choose for them. Parents usually want a child to marry from their own ethnic group, someone like themselves.

Two small churches that met in the same building, but at different hours, considered uniting. One congregation was Czech, the other Dutch. Both held to the same reformed tradition. But one person asked the question, "What if our children should marry someone from the other ethnic group? If our churches join together, this may happen." And that ended all thoughts of uniting in one church.

What should you do when your child brings someone from another background into your family circle? Before marriage, you can point out difficulties inherent in differences. You can help your child see the conflicts ahead, often in most inconsequential matters. He'll discover differences in eating habits, in spending habits. He'll come up against strange attitudes toward chores in the home, toward authority in the home. Who's in charge of what? Different backgrounds can produce totally opposite ideas of a husband-and-wife relationship.

But the Bible marks only one important difference, to be avoided at all costs. "Be ye not unequally yoked together with unbelievers" (2 Cor. 6:14). Did these sons of Naomi insist on their wives accepting their God before marriage? We don't know.

At any rate, after Mahlon and Chilion had married Ruth and Orpah, their mother did the only sensible thing. She accepted them. She not only accepted them as part of her household, but truly loved them. They obviously felt her love and responded.

Said one jolly mother-in-law, in the hearing of one son's wife, "I don't know whether my daughters-in-law love me. But I do know how much I love them. And I also know that if you love somebody they're likely to love you back. So I just don't worry about it." The daughter-in-law who was present grinned appreciatively.

Naomi didn't remind her daughters-in-law daily that they were not her choice. Many of us can glorify God by accepting relationships which are less than ideal.

". . . for she had heard in the country of Moab how that the Lord had visited His people in giving them bread" (1:6).

As Naomi and her two daughters-in-law faced the desolation of widowhood, they received some news from far-off Bethlehem. Things were looking up there. The famine had ended. The good news seemed like cold waters to a thirsty soul (Prov. 25:25). Naomi decided to go back to her own people and her own God.

God tests His people with want. He also summons them with abundance. He visits them in need.

The Hebrew word translated "visited" has no parallel in our language. It means Jehovah has directed His attention to His people. He has inquired into their state, and taken steps to give them bread. The term occurs in various places in the Bible. It tells us something important about the nature of our heavenly Father.

Joseph said to his brothers in Egypt that when he died, God would surely "visit" them. He would bring them out of Egypt (Gen. 50:24).

Four hundred years later God told Moses that He had "visited" His people in Egypt and had seen their afflictions. He would bring them out to a land flowing with milk and honey (Ex. 3:17). When the people realized that God had "visited" them, they believed (Ex. 4:31).

David, the Psalmist, asked, "What is man that Thou art mindful of him? and the son of man, that thou *visitest* him?" (Ps. 8:4) In another psalm he said to God, "Thou hast *visited* me in the night" (Ps. 17:3).

Sometimes in love, God visits with judgments. He says that if His children forsake His Commandments He will "*visit* their transgression with the rod" (Ps. 89:30-32).

But God also visits with redemption. Zacharias rejoiced in the birth of his son, John the Baptist. He said, "Blessed be the Lord God of Israel; for He hath *visited* and redeemed His people" (Luke 1:68).

Naomi hadn't recognized God's hand in withholding bread from Bethlehem. But she did see it when He gave bread. What a tragedy when we fail to recognize God's visitation! Jesus, approaching Jerusalem from the Mount of Olives on that first

Palm Sunday, wept over the City. Said He, "If thou hadst known . . . the things which belong unto thy peace . . . thou knewest not the time of thy *visitation*" (Luke 19:42-44).

"Wherefore she went forth out of the place where she was, and her two daughters-in-law with her; and they went on the way to return unto the land of Judah" (1:7).

Have you ever had to break up a household? When my mother died, my sisters and I faced a sad task. We had to decide what to do with the heirlooms and treasures, the memorabilia carefully saved. We had to divide up or give away the furniture and dishes, the clothing no longer needed. Naomi had to reduce her household to what she could carry. No moving van drove up to transport her belongings.

Naomi's daughters-in-law accompanied her along the dusty trail leading toward the Jordan. The Israelite family apparently had not become naturalized to Moab. No one asked Naomi to stay. No one accompanied her except her daughters-in-law. Apparently Naomi thought they were only intending to walk with her a part of the way.

"And Naomi said unto her two daughters-in-law, 'Go, return each to her mother's house: the Lord deal kindly with you, as ye have dealt with the dead, and with me'" (1:8).

Naomi's attitude toward Orpah and Ruth was unselfish. She appreciated their having made her sons happy. They had shown a gentle spirit as the three women worked together in the home. That wouldn't have come easily, as they would encounter three different ways to grind grain, bake bread, make cheese, or weave cloth.

These three apparently accepted each other as individuals. Each accepted the other's right to do things her own way. They didn't destroy relationships because of trifling differences in taste or procedure.

According to the oriental pattern, Naomi was in charge of the household, yet she must have ruled with a gentle hand. She showed love for her sons when she rejoiced in their happiness, even though that happiness came through other people. Jealousy of in-laws does not spring from love. As the older woman, first responsibility for these good relations lay with Naomi.

Ruth also did her part to create a happy household. She grew up without God, with no knowledge of His ways, yet she adapted to the patterns of this Hebrew household in Moab. She received her husband and his difference in outlook. Naomi, as a foreigner in Moab, must have exhibited habits and customs entirely different from Orpah's and Ruth's. Ruth went into that Hebrew household and accepted Naomi as the ruling woman of the house. She entered into a different way of life.

The mother-daughter-in-law relationship has always been a difficult one. Juvenal, an ancient Roman writer, said, "Domestic concord is impossible as long as the mother-in-law lives." Terence, another Roman writer, said that all mothers-in-law have ever hated their sons' wives. A German proverb states, "The mother-in-law has forgotten that she was ever a daughter-in-law."

Even a modern speaker at a national conference on revival and soul winning joked on the mother-in-law theme. When announcing the offering, he urged people to give "like you were trying to get enough money to send your mother-in-law back home." Yet Ruth and Naomi surmounted the difficulties inherent in their relationship.

Ruth and Orpah must have appreciated the higher morality of a Jewish home. When they married the young Jews from across the Dead Sea, they evidently saw in them something better than they had known. They wanted it enough to face the stigma of marrying foreigners.

In their Moabite homes they were probably familiar with gross immoralities. These were performed even in the name of worship. Despite their background, these girls showed a taste for what was pure and good.

" 'The Lord grant you that ye may find rest, each of you in the house of her husband.' Then she kissed them; and they lifted up their voice and wept" (1:9).

Both girls must have felt overwhelmed by Naomi's loneliness and hunger for their love and companionship. Yet we find Naomi objective enough to look only at their own good. Naomi expressed only one thought for her daughters-in-law—that they find rest. She expresses this in the Hebrew word *menuchah*, which is used throughout the Book of Ruth for marriage. It implies deep peace, protection, harmony, persons in right relation to each other.

The word *menuchah* is also used in Scripture

to mean the rest God offered His people in the Promised Land (Deut. 12:9, 1 Kings 8:56). Jehovah Himself is the *menuchah* of His people (Isa. 32:17-18).

Christ offers the ultimate rest for us all. He promises to give us rest for our souls, and a burden we can easily carry. "Come unto Me, all ye that labor and are heavy laden, and I will give you rest. Take My yoke upon you, and learn of Me, for I am meek and lowly in heart, and ye shall find rest unto your souls. For My yoke is easy, and My burden is light" (Matt. 11:28-30).

Naomi didn't forget Ruth's and Orpah's future in her own need. Nor did she feel they shouldn't marry again. She longed for them to find what she had lost—the security, safety, and honor of a home.

In the time of Ruth, when a woman lost her husband she lost her vocation, her place in life. A woman only became a person as she became a wife. Christ raised women to a whole new level. Married and unmarried women were people to Him. Paul said, "There is neither . . . male nor female, for ye are all one in Christ Jesus" (Gal. 3:28).

Today, a woman can find *menuchah* in a career, in her church, in community service, in friendships and family.

Thelma, grief-stricken over the death of her husband in his forties, found herself alone. She had never lived alone before in her life, and many nights she wept herself to sleep. She held a responsible position as executive secretary in an insurance firm.

She decided that to climb out of her grief she needed a different job. She wanted one that to her seemed more spiritually fulfilling. With three boys to put through college, she couldn't afford to work in a volunteer capacity. She found a job organizing conferences for a Christian organization.

With this job, the intensity of her grief began to abate. She found in her work the rest, the *menuchah,* she needed.

To find rest in our daily lives, we must learn how to give rest. How do you make your home, your church, your place of business, the *menuchah* that you and others need?

Some people by disposition bring *menuchah* to those around them. They feel at rest and peace with themselves; they easily make others around them feel at peace. My mother was such a person. She made rainy days, an ugly house, a penny-pinching life seem beautiful and lovely. She created an aura of restfulness. Everyone who came near felt it.

One woman maintains an aura of peace in a church office—with half a dozen clacking typewriters, telephones, and busy people rushing through. I asked her how she did it.

"I don't really know," she said, "except that I start every day with the Lord. That seems to set an atmosphere that carries through the day, no matter what happens."

All too many homes don't offer the *menuchah* God intended. We can do certain things to create restfulness for those we love.

Each of us offers *menuchah* when we provide security and dependability. A breadwinner gets up every day and goes to work. He uses his paycheck for the good of the whole family. A wife offers *menuchah* when she plans and prepares meals regularly, when she gets the laundry done on time.

The other evening we had dinner in the home of a young couple, both high school teachers. They said they were busy getting their housecleaning done before the school year started. They shared responsibility for their two little children. Each gave the other *menuchah*.

Creating *menuchah* in the home means being willing to blend in and support. It means creating a background against which you and others can become creative. This quality, like humility, is sometimes despised, demeaned, or ignored, regarded like part of the woodwork. Yet it forms a groundwork for growth. Finding and giving *menuchah* involves accepting oneself, one's own role and responsibilities. A wife who fights meals and laundry will never create an atmosphere of restfulness in her home. Domestic life will consist of one crisis after another of lacking necessary food to eat or clothes to wear. A man who runs around with other women will rob himself and his whole family of any semblance of *menuchah*.

Menuchah in the home or church office means accepting other people. You can spend a lifetime trying to increase the speed of a naturally slow person; he won't change a particle. He can't. We must learn to accept people as God has created them. We give *menuchah* to ourselves as we foster an atmosphere that discourages conflict. By our own attitudes we can make standing on rights seem petty.

"And they said unto her, 'Surely we will return with thee unto thy people'" (1:10).

Orpah and Ruth couldn't bear to think of departing

from Naomi. We all find separations painful. This world is a constantly chequered scene of arrivals and departures, with one final departure—death. But as Christians, we look forward to a final re-union, with no more separations.

"And Naomi said, 'Turn again, my daughters: why will ye go with me? Are there yet any more sons in my womb, that they may be your husbands? Turn again, my daughters, go your way; for I am too old to have an husband. If I should say, "I have hope," if I should have an husband also tonight, and should also bear sons; would ye tarry for them till they were grown? Would ye stay for them from having husbands? Nay, my daughters; for it grieveth me much for your sakes that the hand of the Lord is gone out against me'" (1:11-13).

In her extremity of grief, Naomi said many unnecessary things, but refrained from saying what she was really thinking. She could offer Ruth and Orpah no assurance of finding husbands in Bethlehem, because they were Moabite by birth. In going with her, they could expect no prospects except what she herself could offer them.

"And they lifted up their voice and wept again; and Orpah kissed her mother-in-law, but Ruth clave unto her" (1:14).

Orpah went back to her home and her gods. At the critical moment, she lost her resolution. Like many after her, she glimpsed the power of life in Jehovah. Yet she sank back into a world she had half renounced. Her experience parallels what the Apostle

Paul later wrote about a companion: "For Demas hath forsaken me, having loved this present world, and is departed . . ." (2 Tim. 4:10).

But Ruth "clave unto her," literally, "was glued" to her. As a man is to cleave to his wife (Gen. 2:24). As the soul is to follow after and cleave to God (Ps. 63:8; Josh. 23:8). As we are to hold to God's testimonies (Ps. 119:31). As a friend is to stick closer than a brother (Prov. 18:24).

Both daughters-in-law kissed Naomi. Some kisses, like an oceangoing vessel, carry the cargo of a life. Other kisses carry little or no cargo. Some are cheap and sordid. Some even lie. Orpah's expressed a feeling. Ruth's expressed the commitment of a life.

In friendship, in marriage, in Christ, some people go part way—as did Orpah. They reserve the right to abandon you, to take an independent course if it seems the reasonable thing to do. Orpah disappeared with numberless others into the nameless dust of history.

Ruth, who was willing to trust her life to the fortunes of a poor widow, gained everything and became an ancestor of Christ.

3

When Life
Caves In

———————⬤———————

How many partings have you gone through in your lifetime? How many do you foresee having to face?

Naomi had already left father and mother to marry Elimelech. The daughter in that day left her childhood home to live with the family of her husband. It takes some growing up to be married. You have to learn to get along without parents as props.

Another parting for Naomi was cutting all her ties with Bethlehem to go to Moab. She left friends and relatives, and the culture in which she felt at home, and made a life in a foreign country, among strangers.

A young man had always wanted to live in Colorado. Starting out to build his own business, he found a ready market for his skills in Colorado Springs. He moved there with wife and child. But his wife couldn't adjust. She had never lived away from her parents. She missed family and childhood friends. Her unhappiness burdened her husband.

He felt he should move back to the city where they had grown up.

Departures are never easy. In each place you live, you leave a little bit of yourself. We have no evidence that Naomi was ever more than a stranger in Moab. She couldn't become part of that pagan society. She lavished all the love of her heart on husband and sons. Then her husband died.

Said a modern-day widow, "Initially come feelings of shock and merciful numbness. You simply can't take it in that yesterday he was here, today he isn't. Then comes depression, self-pity, and guilt about things you did or didn't do. The Bible says the two shall become one flesh. When death comes, it's like you are cut in two and this feeling lasts for a long time. You are no longer whole, just a left-over half. This is when it is vital you find your own sense of identity."

Naomi found her new sense of identity. She still had her sons. She watched them grow up and take on wives. But she must have experienced some pain in the wives they chose—foreigners.

Then Naomi's sons died. Said a modern couple, grieving together over the death of a child, "Losing a child is the worst. It's worse than losing a mate. You can always marry again, but you can't replace a child." Each person thinks his grief the worst.

In all these bereavements, Naomi enjoyed no New Testament picture of heaven. In most of the Old Testament, we find little understanding of life after death. People believed the soul of every man, good and bad, went to Sheol. Sheol was not a place of torture. But it was a land of the shades, of silence and forgetfulness. Here the dead existed in shadowy, strengthless, joyless lives, like spectres or ghosts. The shades of men were separated from men and God alike.

Said Hezekiah, "The grave cannot praise Thee; death cannot celebrate Thee; they that go down into the pit cannot hope for Thy truth" (Isa. 38:18). (See also Pss. 6:5; 30:9; 88:5, 10-12; 115:17.)

Only occasionally did someone in the Old Testament take a leap of faith. In regard to the afterlife, David said, "My flesh also will dwell securely. For Thou wilt not abandon my soul to Sheol; neither wilt Thou allow Thy Holy One to see the pit. Thou wilt make known to me the path of life; in Thy presence is fulness of joy; in Thy right hand there are pleasures forever" (Ps. 16:9-11, NASB). (See also Ps. 73:23-24; Job 19:25-27.)

Naomi just didn't have the solid faith that we have—"absent from the body . . . present with the Lord" (2 Cor. 5:8). She could only cling blindly to Jehovah in hope and trust. And this she did.

After the death of her sons, Naomi again had to find a new identity. She might have leaned too heavily on daughters-in-law as her only close relatives. Instead, she put her trust in Jehovah. She prepared to turn back to Bethlehem—the land of Jehovah's promises. She was ready to give up her daughters-in-law to reestablish her identity with God's people.

Both daughters-in-law went part way with her. At this point the sorrow of her sons' having married Moabites struck Naomi afresh. Suppose Mahlon and Chilion had married Jewesses. There would be no question of their going back to Israel with Naomi. But because they were Moabites, she had to face parting from these girls she had grown to love.

Strong in her faith in Jehovah, Naomi didn't suffocate Orpah and Ruth with her needs. She appropriated a promise later written into Scripture, "Fear not, for thou . . . shalt not remember the reproach of thy widowhood any more. For thy Maker is thine husband" (Isa. 54:4-5). Now Naomi spoke to Ruth.

"And she said, 'Behold, thy sister-in-law is gone back unto her people, and unto her gods: return thou after thy sister-in-law'" (1:15).

The three had trudged together the dusty trails of Moab high above the Dead Sea. They reached the place where the rolling plateau drops off to the Jordan valley. Here Naomi stopped. If Orpah and Ruth were to go farther, they would have a long climb upward to return. At this point they had to make a full and conscious decision.

Did Naomi want Orpah and Ruth to leave her? Of course not. She advised them unselfishly, from their point of view. She didn't want to swallow up their young lives in her desolation.

Naomi already had reminded the two girls of all they would give up if they continued—parents, homeland, familiar culture, friends. Orpah, like many would-be Christians, turned back. She glimpsed the glories of Israel's God. But consideration of property, pleasure, and her own future persuaded her to return to paganism. Naomi tried to weaken Ruth's resolve by pointing out Orpah's decision. But Ruth refused to be persuaded to return to Moab.

"And Ruth said, 'Entreat me not to leave thee, or

to return from following after thee; for whither thou goest, I will go'" (1:16).

In beautiful words, Ruth expressed undying devotion. The words find a place in many wedding ceremonies. Yet they were spoken to a most unlikely object of love—a mother-in-law.

Ruth met every negative argument Naomi advanced with arguments of her own. Naomi told the two girls she could offer them no home, no security, no *menuchah*. Ruth brushed it all aside with "*where thou lodgest, I will lodge*" (v. 16). The word translated "lodge" means in Hebrew just "stay overnight." It suggests no permanent dwelling place. "You'll be sleeping somewhere," Ruth said in effect. "Wherever you stay, that's where I'll stay. Whatever house you live in will be home to me because you're there." Many wives have made homes out of huts in loyalty to beloved husbands.

Naomi had already warned that the girls would stand out as foreigners in Israel. I grew up in Chicago, where we viewed foreigners with horror. Every so often they appeared in our grade school classes, wearing lumpy stockings, strange caps, and scarves. Big boys had to sit in lower grades, with little kids. They couldn't even speak English. We never thought of how smart they might be in their own language.

Eventually I grew up and traveled about the world. Then I discovered that the "foreigner" is all a matter of where you are. As the foreigner, I often looked stupid amid other people's customs.

Perhaps Naomi didn't want her daughters-in-law to go through what she had experienced. She knew all about being a foreigner in Moab. But Ruth answered that objection: *"Thy people shall be my people"* (v. 16). She had already demonstrated she could accept a foreign husband and mother-in-law. No matter what the difficulties, she would adjust to the people of Bethlehem. She loved Naomi; therefore she would take on a whole new set of human relationships.

Naomi warned that she would have to leave her gods, the dreadful Chemosh and Molech. Ruth had evidently already thought that through and was willing to do so. Naomi's God represented a good part of the reason Ruth wanted to go with Naomi. She had tasted life in a home which worshiped Jehovah. She could not go back to the standards and atmosphere of pagan Moab. Ruth preferred to risk her earthly future. She couldn't give up her one contact with God. *"Thy God, my God,"* (v. 16).

"Where thou diest, will I die, and there will I be buried: the Lord do so to me, and more also, if ought but death part thee and me'" (1:17).

Ruth said, in effect, "I don't care whether you can offer me any kind of life, or not. I'll be content simply to stay with you all your life. I want to be buried where you are." Ruth didn't even desire that her remains be taken back to Moab for burial. And the place of burial was far more important in that day than in ours. She was giving up identification with her ancestors.

Such an avowal of lifelong commitment says a lot about Ruth, and also about Naomi.

Ruth made a choice. André Gide, the French writer, said that choice is terrifying. It sets the pattern of life. So many times choice is final. Once made, we travel the road we have taken. Many times we find no opportunity to turn back. But how wonderful is the power of choice when we choose well.

J. Martin Kohe has written a little book on succeeding in life, called *Your Greatest Power.* He says your greatest power is the power to choose. Ruth chose what she wanted in life. She let no difficulties dissuade her. From her good choice she reaped benefits she never dreamed of.

Robert Frost, the poet, wrote of "The Road Not Taken."

"Two roads diverged in a wood, and I—
I took the one less traveled by,
And that has made all the difference."

Choice presents a terrible responsibility. But it is also terrible not to choose. To fumble and remain in indecision may in itself amount to a choice.

Many times the right choice is lonely. You make it in your heart of hearts, regardless of what others may say or do. Ruth gave up her people, her language, her home, her gods to follow Naomi and Naomi's God. She went alone with Naomi.

Said Joshua in the face of all opposition, "Choose you this day whom ye will serve . . . but as for me and my house, we will serve the Lord" (Josh. 24:15). As a Moabitess, Ruth was probably brought up to hate Israel. Yet love of Mahlon and of Naomi drew her to Israel's God.

"When she saw that she was stedfastly minded to go with her, then she left speaking unto her" (1:18).

When one of my children was sick as a toddler, my

doctor told me to keep him in his crib, up off the floor. I said helplessly, "How can I keep him in his crib? He'll simply climb out."

Said the doctor, "If you make up your mind to keep him in his crib, he'll know it and stay there. Try it, and you'll see." I tried it, and it was true.

We know when a person speaks, even quietly, from determination. We also know when he speaks only tentatively. We could save ourselves a lot of trouble by backing our words with firm determination.

"So they two went until they came to Bethlehem" (1:19).

The two women showed determination in traveling all the way to Bethlehem. They carried what they could of their belongings. Thus burdened, they climbed the desolate trail through the Judean wilderness. They faced dangers of robbers and wild animals along the way. The limestone caves in the lonely hills often sheltered brigands who preyed on travelers. Yet alone and unprotected, Naomi and Ruth persisted. No dangers, no temptations, no weariness stopped them.

Sometimes two who persist in going back to the place of spiritual blessing are husband and wife. Sometimes two sisters return, or two friends, or parent and child. We love to read the words of Ruth's beautiful resolve. We also thrill to see it carried out. At last, Ruth and Naomi rounded a turn in the hills. They sighted the limestone houses of Bethlehem in the distance.

The road to Bethlehem follows a ridge of mountains. Villagers must have spotted the two women as they approached. They wore strange attire, and traveled alone. They looked worn from their journey. We might have detected a bit of gloating as the women viewed Naomi with interest and surprise.

"And it came to pass, when they were come to Bethlehem, that all the city was moved about them, and they said, 'Is this Naomi?'" (1:19)

Naomi went out a blooming matron, a substantial citizen of the town. Elimelech and Naomi could afford to make a move, to try their fortunes elsewhere. Now the people who stayed and suffered through the famine noticed how much worse Naomi appeared to have fared than they.

Some years ago I visited third cousins of mine in Scotland. Throughout our visit they debated, "Did your grandparents, or ours make the better choice? Should our grandparents have emigrated to the United States as yours did?" My cousins wanted to persuade themselves their family did better by staying in Scotland.

The women of Bethlehem wanted to assure themselves they had made the better choice by staying. There's always a temptation to mark the mistakes made by people who find themselves in trouble. Those in Bethlehem felt a little smug. They saw Naomi aged, wrinkled, dressed in widow's garb. She had only a Moabite woman as a companion.

Whatever Naomi's mistakes, we see in her life how God can overrule mistakes. He can make out of the wreckage of life a beautiful thing—if we let Him. Among the villagers we detect no welcome, no warmth, no help for Naomi and Ruth. Toward Ruth they felt the natural resentment of foreigners.

"And she said unto them, 'Call me not Naomi [pleasantness], call me Mara [bitterness]: for the Almighty hath dealt very bitterly with me. I went out full, and the Lord hath brought me home again empty: why then call ye me Naomi, seeing the Lord hath testified against me, and the Almighty hath afflicted me?'" (1:20-21)

Naomi's griefs swept over her afresh as she met former acquaintances. Grief often comes in waves. Naomi met the unhelpful attitude of the women with an outburst of self-pity. Her words may have seemed out of character for the patient sufferer she was. Yet even in this moment she assumed full responsibility for her actions. She didn't blame her dead husband. "*I* went out full." Memory colored recollections. She hardly went out full. She left because of famine. Only now did she realize what riches she possessed at that time in the form of a husband and two sons. In this moment of self-pity Naomi's concern for Ruth lapsed. She called herself "empty"—yet there stood patient Ruth at her side.

Naomi attributed all her sorrows to God. This isn't exactly true, because some things we bring upon ourselves. This is a moral universe. Certain results follow from choices we make.

God allows evils to follow bad choices in order to bring us back to Himself. We have to distinguish between God's permissive will and His directive will. We see in Naomi's life how all things can work together for good to those who love God, to those who are the called according to His purpose (Rom. 8:28). Ruth was the greatest good to come out of Naomi's life in Moab.

Perhaps of all Naomi's griefs, the worst moment

came when she felt God had forsaken her. *El Shaddai,* meaning "the One who provides," is the term used here. In selfish moments of grief, we stand in a house of mirrors. Every way we look we see only ourselves. Yet even in grief God offers us windows. Through windows we can gaze out on peaks of inspirations, lakes of beauty. We can discover fields in life to be cultivated.

The deceased was young and the family grief-stricken. Bart, young himself, was to officiate at the funeral. He didn't know the family. A middle-aged woman was comforting them. Bart saw love flowing from her to the sorrowing. He asked her, "How are you so helpful at a time like this?"

She replied, "A few years ago my family and I suffered a terrible auto accident. My husband died instantly. Two children were killed. I held my dead baby in my arms. Then I slipped into unconsciousness. When I became aware and knew what had happened, I did not want to live. God enfolded me in His loving arms and consoled me. He said to me, 'You can use your grief to destroy yourself or to bless others. You can comfort others bereaved.' This I have chosen to do. I tell them my story. They reach out for Christ's comfort."

"So Naomi returned, and Ruth the Moabitess, her daughter-in-law, with her, which returned out of the country of Moab: and they came to Bethlehem in the beginning of barley harvest" (1:22).

Naomi and Ruth came back to pick up Naomi's old life at a moment of opportunity. The year's fresh crop of barley was waving in the breeze in the fields below Bethlehem. It was April. The winter was over and past, the time of the singing of birds had come.

Sometimes grief blinds us to opportunities. We watch to see if Naomi and Ruth will make the most of their moment for action.

"There is a tide in the affairs of men,
Which, taken at the flood, leads on to fortune;
Omitted, all the voyage of their life
Is bound in shallows and in miseries."

(Shakespeare, *Julius Caesar,*
act 4, scene 3)

4

Face the Worst First

Enter the hero of our story, Boaz. Who was he? What was he like? Because Ruth faced the worst first, she and Boaz met.

"And Naomi had a kinsman of her husband's, a mighty man of wealth, of the family of Elimelech; and his name was Boaz" (2:1).

In those days people often acquired names that described their characteristics. Boaz' name means fleetness, alacrity, strength. The name sounds like he was one of those people who knew how to do things—someone who worked and acted fast and effectively.

We learn something else about Boaz right away. He was a kinsman of Naomi's husband. Does that mean he was in the line of potential kinsmen-redeemers—one of whom could redeem the property and family of Elimelech if he chose to? The word for the one who redeems is *goel* in Hebrew.

The word used about Boaz, though translated kinsman, is only *moda*—acquaintance or friend. Yet Boaz was of the family of Elimelech, perhaps a distant relationship.

Quite often widows or widowers marry a close friend of the deceased partner—an arrangement that often works out well. You can talk to the new mate about him or her. You don't have to act as if the first husband or wife never existed.

A certain young woman, tall and willowy, married a stalwart young man. Selecting with utmost care, she waited till age 28 to become engaged and married. For two years she revelled in her happiness. Then her husband developed a serious disease. After months of suffering, he died. She was devastated with grief. Her husband's best friend, who stood up for him at their wedding, came to comfort her. In a few months they were married. They lived happily ever after—for some 30 years now.

An aunt of mine died in her sixties, after a long and happy marriage. Said she to her husband, in her final illness, "If you must marry someone after I'm gone, why don't you choose someone nice—like Mary?" Mary, her friend for many years, lived in the same small town.

My uncle did. He and Mary moved smoothly and easily into a few years of wedded happiness. No crises of adjustment. No shocks or surprises.

We learn something else about Boaz in these few words. He was "a mighty man of wealth," suggested by the single Hebrew word *gibbor*. Elsewhere *gibbor* suggests different qualities. It is translated "mighty man of valor" in regard to Gideon and Jephthah (Jud. 6:12; 11:1). The very same word is applied to Ruth (3:11). There it is translated "a virtuous woman," or "woman of excellence" (NASB), or "a woman of strength—worth, bravery, capability" (AMP). A passage in Isaiah uses the word in describing Messiah: "For unto us a child is born, unto us a son is given . . . His name shall be called Wonderful, Counselor, *The mighty God* (El gibbor) . . ." (Isa. 9:6). Here *gibbor* refers to Messiah as the bodily presence of the strong God.

What does it all add up to in regard to Boaz? The word originally meant strength, then valor. From the idea of valor developed the meaning of a clannish following. Then *gibbor* came to be used of a military host, or force or forces. From that idea it took on the meaning of faculty or ability. Then it came to mean riches or wealth. So the single word *gibbor* suggests many things about Boaz. People viewed him as a strong and substantial man.

Throughout the centuries, believers have seen Boaz as a type of Christ. We know Christ as the source of strength. "I can do all things through Christ who strengthens me" (Phil. 4:13, SCO.). What qualities did Boaz have in common with Christ? Let's notice, as the story develops.

Ruth and Naomi had suffered the stress of change. We all encounter change in one way or another. A fall from affluence because of retirement or job loss. Bereavement. Accident. Stroke. Divorce. Earthquake. Typhoon. Tornado. Serious illness of a loved one. Any one of these events leaves you never the same afterward.

Ruth and Naomi had to cope with change. A brokendown house needed repair. Limestone walls might still stand solid. The roof, probably formed of branches and earth, would certainly need reconstruction. They would have to clean out the dust of more than 10 years. And they had nothing to eat in the house. No one planted crops the fall before on their family plot of ground. The rainy season, just past, produced no grain belonging to them.

People react in different ways to difficulties. Some go numb, and let others take care of them. Ruth shared all of Naomi's changes—plus culture shock. Yet, Ruth came up with an idea.

"And Ruth the Moabitess said to Naomi, 'Please let me go to the field and glean among the ears of grain after one in whose sight I may find favor.' And she said to her, 'Go, my daughter'" (2:2, NASB).

Gleaning meant picking up stray bits of grain overlooked by paid field workers. The Old Testament law designated gleaning as a means of aid to the very poor. Going out to glean meant that socially and financially you had reached bottom.

Gleaning constituted a sound plan of providing for the poor. It offered necessary help without weakening the capacity for work. It solved a problem we haven't unraveled in the welfare tangle to this day.

Apparently, Ruth knew the Israelite law of gleaning. Fatherless, a stranger, and a widow, she held a triple claim to gleanings. "And when ye reap the harvest of your land, thou shalt not wholly reap the corners of thy field, neither shalt thou gather the gleanings of thy harvest. And thou shalt not glean thy vineyard, neither shalt thou gather every grape of thy vineyard; thou shalt leave them for the poor and stranger; I am the Lord your God" (Lev. 19:9-10).

An article in the *Wall Street Journal* describes a modern gleaning operation. A self-help society of oldsters in California became interested in gleaning. They obtained permission from farmers, food-producers, and handlers to gather food that would otherwise go to waste. Members of the organization gather from the fields what machinery or professional pickers miss. They manage to fill their own freezers and share with others too feeble to work.

Moses repeated the instruction about gleaning just before the Israelites entered the Promised Land. A sheaf forgotten in the field "shall be for the stranger, for the fatherless, and for the widow" (Deut. 24:19).

Yet it must have shocked Naomi for Ruth to propose that she go out and glean. Anyone who has enjoyed a position of giving doesn't enjoy having to receive from others.

Ruth might have said, "If gleaning is all I can find to do in Israel, I'm going back to Moab." But she didn't. She stuck by her decision, she faced facts, she accepted realities. She wasted no energy worrying about her image in the town.

A young man once built up a good business of his own as supplier of parts for the automobile industry. Because of changes in production patterns, his business went under. Not finding other work, he took a job as a common laborer in building construction. Doing the best he could with pick and shovel he was soon promoted to foreman. We all admire the person who accepts disappointment and works at the job available. Ruth didn't set up any false barriers to action.

Often the hardest part of a job is starting. Who of us hasn't faced an overwhelming task of cleaning basement, garage, or doing yard work? Mothers of small children know that if they just relax for a couple of hours, the house is in chaos, and they can hardly face getting it to rights. If you think in terms of the whole job, you can't move. If you start by putting one item in its place, you can proceed.

The other day I was trying to get into the mood to write a chapter of a book. I didn't think I could do much at it that day. So many other things had occupied my mind. But in turning over ideas, words for the first paragraph popped into my head. I thought, "I'll just type the first paragraph today." Before I quit, I'd written most of the chapter. "A task begun is half done," says the old proverb.

Ruth didn't hesitate about starting. She didn't try to outwit Naomi. As a foreigner, Ruth might have figured she didn't know local customs. She should stay home and keep house, let Naomi go out and glean. But she didn't. Instead, she asked very sweetly for Naomi's permission. She stood ready to undertake the hard job.

Several centuries ago, Edward Young said, "Procrastination is the thief of time." How do you fight your tendency to procrastinate? I fight mine by making lists. Crossing off the easy things encourages me every so often to face a hard thing. Eventually I even do things I hate to do, just to get them off the list.

Ruth didn't need any list to remind her to glean. She faced the urgency of no food in the house. But she could have found excuses for delay. "He that observeth the wind shall not sow; and he that regardeth the clouds shall not reap" (Ecc. 11:4).

"And she went, and came, and gleaned in the field after the reapers: and her hap was to light on a part of the field belonging unto Boaz, who was of the kindred of Elimelech" (2:3).

Dressed in working clothes one spring morning, Ruth walked down the hillside. She headed for the great field of grain occupying the valley below Bethlehem. No walls, hedges, or fences separated one man's portion of the field from another's. Only a stone or little pile of stones every rod or so marked boundaries. These proved scarcely visible in the waving grain.

Ruth heard the rustle of reapers' sickles. Behind the reapers she saw women binding the cut grain into handfuls of sheaves. She asked the servant in charge of some reapers if she might glean in his field. The servant, knowing his master's policy in regard to gleaners, granted permission.

Ruth "happened" to come to Boaz' field? The outcome of that one happening determined her marriage, her future, and that of Naomi. It resulted in Ruth's position in history as ancestress of Christ.

One noontime some years ago, my husband and I attended a missionary luncheon in a hotel banquet room. We were in New York being briefed for a three-month preaching and teaching mission to the Philippines. I wanted very much to go with my husband and teach the Bible, yet I wasn't at all sure I could stand up to the trip. Low blood sugar had partially incapacitated me; most doctors then didn't understand the problem.

A woman coming late to the luncheon walked past several hundred people in that vast room. She sat down next to me. I soon learned she was a medical missionary serving in India. I told her about my worries. It turned out she herself also suffered from hypoglycemia! She told me things about diet (high protein, frequent meals) and vitamins (lots of B vitamins). Her helpfulness lifted me to a whole new level of health—for that trip and ever since. She explained how to manage the diet while traveling.

Before parting, she told me how she happened to sit next to me. As she entered the room, she asked God to guide her to someone she could help. I've always believed He directed that doctor to sit in the chair next to mine. God guided Ruth to a particular plot in that vast field below Bethlehem.

"And behold, Boaz came from Bethlehem, and said unto the reapers, 'The Lord be with you.' And they answered him, 'The Lord bless thee'" (2:4).

Boaz, as owner, seemed to take friendly interest in those he employed. He brought the mention of God into his employer-employee relations. Perhaps respect for God's standards is what is lacking in most struggles between employers and workers today. The Bible instructs workers to do their very best to produce. It tells employers to share generously with workers. If individuals followed these principles, most disputes would melt away. (For instruction to workers, see Eph. 6:5-8; Col. 3:22-25. For instruction to employers, see Eph. 6:9, and Col. 4:1.)

The Lincoln Electric Company of Cleveland, Ohio, has never suffered a strike because management and labor work together instead of against each other. A friend of ours is employed by the company. He works hard, his wife says, but work for him isn't the hassle it is for most people in business.

The concept of "incentive management" at the company was started in the 1930s by James F. Lincoln. At that time he allowed each worker to buy into the company. Employees share in profits, and vote in many decisions. The company pays cash for improvements, and divides up year-end profits among all regular employees.

The customer shares in profits too. An electric welding machine sold 20 years ago for $200. Today it sells for $120. The drive toward greater efficiency on the part of every employee in the company makes such price reductions possible.

Every permanent employee earns a salary—a guaranteed annual income. In addition, each so far has always received a good bonus. The company hasn't fired anybody in many years, and people seldom quit. Productivity per worker amounts to two to three times the average in a similar industry.

By popular vote, even management works amidst meager furnishings. The president and vice-presidents work in cubicles, not private offices. No thick carpets, or luxurious furniture are displayed as status symbols. Anyone can go to the president with a problem or an idea for better productivity.

Labor organizations have tried unsuccessfully to organize Lincoln Electric workers against management. But these workers enjoy too many benefits from working *with* management. They refuse to organize as labor.

The company, with 2,400 employees, is studied at Harvard and in most business school curriculums. The National Broadcasting Company featured it in a documentary on labor and management relations. The implication: perhaps labor and management don't have to suffer the terrible clashes we see so often.

In the Book of Ruth, we see Boaz' concern for his workers. Fringe benefits included a shelter for rest, water to drink when thirsty.

Boaz, with friendly involvement, set the atmosphere for his workers. Today, no amount of money will make up to workers for an ugly emotional environment. Why not make the day's work happy for others?

Living out the truth of God in labor relations prevents wrong use of power by management. It also prevents laziness or insubordination on the part of workers.

"Then said Boaz unto his servant that was set over the reapers, 'Whose damsel is this?'" (2:5)

In the midst of the happy harvesting scene, Boaz saw Ruth. She attracted his interest right away. "Whose damsel?" he asked. Was she married? If not, whose daughter? A new girl on the scene! Ruth must have possessed a special bearing, perhaps an exotic beauty which commanded Boaz' attention.

"And the servant that was set over the reapers answered and said, 'It is the Moabitish damsel

that came back with Naomi out of the country of
Moab: And she said, "I pray you, let me glean and
gather after the reapers among the sheaves": so
she came, and hath continued even from the morn-
ing until now, that she tarried a little in the house'"
(2:6-7).

The servant gave the information sought. And he
mentioned twice in his brief remarks that she was
a foreigner. But Ruth evidently had won the servant's respect. He mentioned that she had asked
politely if she might glean in Boaz' plot of ground.
The overseer was impressed that she had stuck to
the hard job. He noted she spent little time resting
in the hut or tent. Or perhaps the shelter was a
booth constructed of branches and leaves to protect from the sun.

Naomi had to win her way back into the affections of her kinsmen and neighbors. Ruth had to
overcome their prejudice against a foreigner, to
find acceptance in Bethlehem. Already we see her
succeeding. Apparently the overseer and Boaz both
knew about her. Yet Boaz saw her now for the first
time.

So far in our Book of Ruth, we have seen outstanding relationships already glowing with beauty.
New relationships are about to spring into ex-
istence.

5

How to Attract Attention

———————●———————

Every child bursts into the world crying for attention. He experiments with right and wrong ways to gain the recognition he requires.

Ruth came to Bethlehem as a foreigner, widowed and poverty-stricken. She demonstrated for us some right ways to gain favorable attention, in a difficult situation.

"Then Boaz said unto Ruth, 'Hearest thou not, my daughter? Go not to glean in another field, neither go from hence, but abide here fast by my maidens'" (2:8).

Boaz' kind words must have sounded to Ruth like desert springs of water. He invited her to continue to glean in his field. He even urged her to keep close to the girls who tied up his grain in sheaves. There she would find more grain than if she stayed back with the gleaners.

So far as the record goes, these constitute the first

words of encouragement for Ruth. She had tasted plenty of sorrow. She suffered at the grave of her husband. She must have suffered in parting from her parents and the land of her birth. She certainly didn't receive any big welcome in Bethlehem. As far as we know, the women who met her and Naomi didn't address any remarks at all to Ruth. And everyone spoke of her as "the Moabitess." The people of Bethlehem seemed never to forget for an instant that she was a foreigner.

Now for the first time someone said to her, "Stay, draw near, don't go anywhere else."

Jesus says to each of us, "Abide with Me. Stay close" (John 15). He wants us to do our harvesting close to Him—as Boaz wanted Ruth to glean the food she needed in his field and no other.

Boaz wasn't afraid to take on another dependent. He wasn't looking for what he could get from Ruth, but rather what he could give. What are you looking for in your relationships? What you can give? Or what you can get?

Ruth must have recognized in Boaz' words another step in God's guidance. Here the owner, Boaz, not only followed Old Testament law for allowing gleaners on his property. In his provisions for Ruth, he went far beyond what the law required.

You and I can look for God's guiding hand in the little things of life. An open door of circumstances or an encouraging word may beckon us into some path of God's choosing. At other times we need to accept closed doors and discouraging words; these may indicate we should look elsewhere. Many romances have blossomed from seemingly accidental meetings. Many business opportunities have sprung from small happenings.

Think back. Where do you see God's guiding hand in your life? What seemingly chance happening determined a direction? What little event resulted in your coming to Christ? Did you see God's hand in it at the time? In what ways did God guide you in lesser matters?

"*'Let thine eyes be on the field that they do reap, and go thou after them: have I not charged the young men that they shall not touch thee? And when thou art athirst, go unto the vessels, and drink of that which the young men have drawn'*" (2:9).

Boaz welcomed Ruth with openhanded hospitality. He offered her water to drink. Today we wouldn't count water as a gift, because it doesn't cost us anything. But this water cost Boaz; it had to be drawn up from a well, one jar or bucketful at a time. He ordered a servant to draw it up for his workers. No landowner could be expected to provide water for gleaners. Yet Boaz offered it to Ruth.

Boaz also provided for Ruth's mental comfort as part of his hospitality. He warned the young men who cut grain not to touch her. Like young men of any day, they might have made approaches to her as an attractive girl. In that society they might have considered her fair prey. She was only a foreigner without husband or father.

Boaz treated Ruth as God wanted His people to treat all strangers. God made clear in the law that He wanted strangers treated hospitably. Israelites were to remember they were once strangers in the land of Egypt (Ex. 22:21; 23:9; Lev. 19:34) and in Canaan (Ex. 6:4).

In the New Testament also, God gave a big place to hospitality. Jesus said we take Him in every time we share with a stranger, with "one of the least of these My brethren" (Matt. 25:40).

When my son was a college student, he took a trip through Germany. A cousin I grew up with, but hadn't seen in years, was spending a year there. She took Dan in and entertained him warmly. I felt she had done it for me.

We're to entertain strangers, says the writer of Hebrews, for we might someday find we have entertained an angel without realizing it (Heb. 13:2). Suppose Boaz had run his farm with a tightfisted policy of keeping all produce for himself. He would have missed finding Ruth.

The smallest gesture can warm the heart of a stranger so much. In the Philippines, my husband and I were walking about the town of Tayug. We found ourselves the only white people to visit the town in six months. As such we became an enormous curiosity. A throng of children followed us every time we appeared on the street. They liked to watch us and listen to our strange talk. They knew a little English, so we could converse some.

Coming to a stream across our path, Bart and I started to turn back. We didn't want to get our shoes wet. But those children and young people splashed into the stream in their rubber sandals. They began building a little causeway with rocks. Then they held us each by the hand to help us balance; we walked across the stream on the rocks they placed for us. Such a little gesture—but so enormously heartwarming to us as strangers in the town.

Another time, while we were traveling with our

children on Prince Edward Island, we attended church in Charlottetown. A woman sitting behind us tapped us on the shoulder at the end of the service. Inviting us for dinner, she said, "I don't cook on Sunday, and it's really only a lunch, but we'd like you to share it with us." We would gladly have shared a piece of bread with her.

Many of us make too big a deal of entertaining. Boaz simply invited Ruth to share what he had. True hospitality means simply sharing. It is not building up to some big occasion whereby we may impress people. Is your entertaining a matter of display and selfish pride? Or do you, like Boaz, simply share what you have and are?

"Then she fell on her face, and bowed herself to the ground, and said unto him, 'Why have I found grace in thine eyes, that thou shouldest take knowledge of me, seeing I am a stranger?'" (2:10)

What's happening? It looks like some great attraction is detaining the busy man of affairs.

Probably scarcely a marriage takes place but someone wonders, "What does she see in him?" or "What does he see in her?" At one wedding a friend of the bride asked, "Do you think he's good enough for her?" To this question a friend of the groom answered, "We who are his friends wonder if she's good enough for him."

Any of the townsfolk would have understood what Ruth saw in Boaz. He probably stood out as the town's most eligible bachelor or widower. More difficult for them to see would be what attracted him to her.

In this verse we glimpse some of Ruth's charms.

We see her humility. The minute Boaz spoke to her, she might have fallen into explaining. She could have said she wasn't used to gleaning, she came from a higher station in life. She might have complained about the hardships to which circumstances had reduced her.

Instead Ruth expressed simple gratitude. Difficulty in expressing gratitude may come from lack of emotional development. In her readiness to express thanks, Ruth evidenced a rich emotional life.

She showed respect for Boaz as she dropped to her knees, touched her forehead to the ground. In whatever way our society requires, we're to show respect for every person. "Honor all men. Love the brotherhood. Fear God. Honor the king" (1 Peter 2:17). Respect for another personality forms the base on which to build any relationship.

Hans, a young professor of philosophy, might play the part of the snobbish intellectual. Instead, he shows outstanding ability to relate to all kinds of people. I questioned him about this one time. Said he, "I genuinely respect every person as a child of God."

Ruth also expressed a childlike wonder as she spoke to Boaz. She didn't take his attention for granted. She didn't feel the world—or Boaz—owed her a living. Some people weary us with demands of what they consider their due. Such pressure makes us feel like giving less rather than more.

Many of God's great people have expressed the same wonder at being noticed. Moses marveled that he should be chosen to bring Israel out of Egypt (Ex. 3:11). David wondered that God should raise him to the kingship (2 Sam. 7:18). Paul didn't consider himself worthy of preaching the unsearchable riches of Christ (Eph. 3:8). Ruth took nothing for granted for the future. She mentioned only the miracle of Boaz' having noticed her at all. Carlisle wrote that every person should put himself at zero; then he should receive everything that comes to him as an occasion of gratitude.

The Bible makes clear how we're to go about attracting the attention we crave. We're not to depend upon outward adorning, but on "the hidden man of the heart . . . a meek and quiet spirit, which is in the sight of God of great price" (1 Peter 3:4). God deplores those who put all their emphasis upon artificial aids to beauty. In Isaiah 3:16-26 He mentions a list of ornaments that sound ridiculous to us. Ours might sound equally ridiculous to later generations.

"And Boaz answered and said unto her, 'It hath fully been showed me, all that thou hast done unto thy mother-in-law since the death of thine husband: and how thou hast left thy father and thy mother, and the land of thy nativity, and art come unto a people which thou knewest not heretofore'" (2:11).

Boaz knew all about Ruth's kindness to her mother-in-law—just as Christ knows all about us. In the little town of Bethlehem, Boaz would readily hear of Ruth. Yet knowledge of Ruth's character must have come ultimately from Naomi's own lips.

God values such unselfish love as that of Ruth and Naomi and Boaz. The Book of Ruth teaches reconciliation—building relationships across chasms of difficulty. Boaz exhibited godliness when he respected Ruth for her loving care of Naomi. To Boaz, character counted more than background.

Boaz also admired Ruth's courage and independence in choosing to live in his country. Her
appreciation for Israelite culture formed a basis
for relationship. We endear ourselves to people
anywhere as we appreciate the place where they
live.

Imagine how Boaz' words must have strength-
ened Ruth. She may have supposed no one noticed
her quiet faithfulness to duty. Boaz' words spurred
her to even greater efforts to please Naomi. We
can help people working at obscure tasks by voic-
ing appreciation for what they're doing.

Boaz learned about and appreciated Ruth. Christ
knows all about us. Miraculously, He still loves
us.

Some people moan that they want to be appreciated for themselves, not for what they do. But
what we do expresses what we are. Our deeds go
before us, making a way for us. How would Boaz
have known about the sterling qualities of Ruth if
she hadn't acted? She translated feelings into
action. Her actions have lived long after her.

*"The Lord recompense thy work, and a full re-
ward be given thee of the Lord God of Israel,
under whose wings thou art come to trust"* (2:12).

Boaz saw accurately into Ruth's heart. He understood her great forsaking, her great choice, her
great embracing. He felt that God should reward
Ruth for her trust in Him. Curiously, Boaz himself
would prove the answer to his own prayers for
Ruth. How many times have you found yourself
the answer to your prayers for someone else? For
your church? For a need in your community?

Boaz was sensitive to Ruth's anxiety and isolation. He grasped her difficulty in adjusting to life in a new culture. He did not address her as a rich person speaking to a charity case. Nor did he converse with Ruth as a distant relative. He spoke here as a priest of Jehovah, rejoicing that she had come to trust under God's wings. Boaz knew God as a God of rewards. He understood that God's rewards depend upon our trust.

Trusting God doesn't always bring outward rewards in this life. But it does always bring the supreme reward of Christ's presence. Jesus, with the Father and the Spirit, will make His abode with one who loves and trusts Him (John 14:23). The greatest reward is just knowing Christ, sharing His sufferings, entering into His death (Phil. 3:10).

But many times we do receive rewards in this life. The fruit of the Spirit pleases God. We're to produce love, joy, peace, longsuffering, gentleness, goodness, faith, meekness, hope. As we show these qualities toward others, we tend to get the same attitudes back. As with Ruth, simple goodness enables us to build good relationships. These become their own reward.

One time, my husband was called early in the morning to the bedside of a young man dying of kidney trouble. For four or five hours Bart sat with the young wife while death overtook her husband. Their baby had died only a few months before. She told Bart that a friend of hers had also lost husband and child. This friend ended in a mental institution.

Bart said, "You can go the way of your friend, or you can take hold of the strength of God. I suggest after John has gone, that you busy yourself in the church. You can reach out to other people, find a new life for yourself."

The young woman, whose name also happened to be Ruth, did. She joined the choir and taught a Sunday School class, while working as a secretary. She loved the children she taught so much that she decided to become a school teacher.

She went away to a state university to get her degree. There she met a young man a few years younger than herself. They became engaged and married, and brought up two children. This Ruth felt God restored to her all she had lost. But her beautiful spirit attracted to herself the rewards God wanted to give her.

Boaz rejoiced in Ruth's coming to trust under "the wings of Jehovah." This vivid figure of God's wings as protection appears many times in the Bible. God told Moses to tell Israel how He had borne them "on eagles' wings, and brought you unto Myself" (Ex. 19:4). By strength of its powerful wings an eagle can carry quite a load with its feet. The psalmist spoke many times of God's wings as a refuge. "Under His wings shalt thou trust" (Ps. 91:4. See also Pss. 17:8; 36:7-8; 57:1-2; 61:4; 63:7).

When Christ grieved over Jerusalem, He used the figure of the hen's protection of her chicks. She fluffs out her feathers and clucks to call her little ones. She gathers them under her wings for safety and comfort (Matt. 23:37-38). The mother hen never uses compulsion, as does a mother dog or cat. She only calls. She clucks a cheery call to dinner, to feed on the good things of life. She clucks to warn of danger. She clucks to call the tired chicks to rest. And she clucks to her chicks under her wings with the pure enjoyment of motherhood.

God's wings can bring to us the healing of righteousness (Mal. 4:2). Boaz rejoiced that Ruth had sought her refuge under the wings of Jehovah. He addressed her as a fellow believer.

"Then she said, 'Let me find favor in thy sight, my lord; for that thou hast comforted me, and for that thou hast spoken friendly unto thine [literally, to the heart of your] *handmaid, though I be not like unto one of thine handmaidens'"* (2:13).

Ruth showed no consciousness of having done anything special. She supposed Boaz to be equally kind to others.

"And Boaz said unto her, 'At mealtime come thou hither, and eat of the bread, and dip thy morsel in the vinegar.' And she sat beside the reapers: and he reached her parched corn, and she did eat, and was sufficed, and left" (2:14).

Laborers in the vineyard enjoyed the sour wine or fermented acid drink offered to Ruth. They ate wheat as "parched corn," before it was fully ripe. It was roasted in a pan over the fire. Ruth ate and was satisfied. Christ offers us all the spiritual food we need. We too can eat and become satisfied. Close to Boaz, Ruth found many good gifts, beyond what she looked for. As we keep close to Christ, we find good things beyond our imagining.

"And when she was risen up to glean, Boaz commanded his young men, saying, 'Let her glean

*even among the sheaves, and reproach her not:
and let fall also some of the handfuls of purpose
for her, and leave them, that she may glean them,
and rebuke her not'"* (2:15-16).

However much Ruth impressed Boaz, he didn't tell
her to stop gleaning. He didn't say she was too
good for such work. Rather, by making her gleaning more rewarding, he encouraged her to continue. He now wanted her to glean even among
the sheaves. In so doing, Boaz went far beyond the
bounds of generosity and compassion for the poor.
These instructions showed he felt a peculiar interest in Ruth. He had charged the young men not to
touch her. Now he charged them not to rebuke her.
They were not to shame her by referring to her
nationality. Neither were they to twit her about
the special favors being shown her.

I love the "handfuls of purpose" of the King
James version. Actually, the Hebrew suggests more
in the action than "let fall." The reapers were actually to draw out grain for her from the bundles.
They were deliberately to leave grain for her to
glean. At the same time they were to find no fault
with her for taking so much. Thus Boaz protected
Ruth's pride. He made her increase appear to be
the result of her own hard work. We can learn
from him about how to give to someone in need.

Thus Ruth came to trust under the wings of
Jehovah. Boaz accepted her. Their coming together
breathed the spirit of God's salvation for all. God
wanted Israel to witness to Gentiles. He wanted
Gentiles like Ruth to come. We notice the mounting
series of extras that came to Ruth. They came after
her decision to go God's way.

When we act by faith, God gives abundant confirmation. He blesses us along the way. We have all seen God's "handfuls of purpose" in our lives.

Have you trusted God? If so, what special "handfuls of purpose" has He given to you?

6

You
and Your Work

————————⚫————————

Starting a hard job is very difficult for some people. For others, starting is nothing compared to finishing. Who of us hasn't left behind a few carcasses of projects we started but never finished? After a number of years, you just clear such things out of the house. You resolve to weigh carefully what you start in the future.

Ruth started the difficult job of gleaning with eagerness. She finished the first day's work, and also the season's work. By starting, she attracted Boaz' attention. By the time she finished, she had won his heart. Time passed between the beginning of barley harvest in April and the end of wheat harvest four weeks later in May. The time gave romance a chance to develop. For all those days, Boaz saw her in the field. He sat with her at meals, found opportunities to seek her out. An electrical attraction drew them to each other.

"So she gleaned in the field until even, and beat

*out that she had gleaned: and it was about an
ephah of barley"* (2:17).

As the first gleaning drew to its close, Ruth must
have felt awful weariness. Yet one job remained
if she wanted to complete her work. No use trying
to carry all that straw home along with the grain.
She might as well beat it out here and leave the
straw in the field. So she took a stick or stone to
beat with. Or she used a suitable rod or simple
flail she had brought with her. Perhaps she secured
one from the threshing hut. Tired as she was, she
worked over the barley. At last she could gather
up the grain in her shawl for carrying home.

Ruth must have felt satisfaction as she saw the
mound increasing. She lifted the load and trudged
happily home. Its heaviness told her how much
she'd accomplished. Her hard work brought her
the joy of achievement.

The Bible gives a big place to work and its satisfactions. "Six days shalt thou labor and do all thy
work . . ." (Ex. 20:9). God designates only one
day for rest. Work appears to be man's natural
state. The Lord God put the man "into the garden
of Eden to dress it and to keep it."

The Book of Proverbs says a lot about work.
"Go to the ant, thou sluggard; consider her ways,
and be wise . . . Yet a little sleep, a little slumber,
a little folding of the hands to sleep: So shall thy
poverty come . . ." (Prov. 6:6, 10-11. See also
Prov. 10:4-5; 12:11, 24, 27; 13:4, 11, 23; 14:4, 23;
16:26; 20:13; 21:5; 27:23; 28:19; 30:25-26.) The
virtuous woman is described as looking well to the
ways of her household. She doesn't eat the bread
of idleness (Prov. 31:27). That was Ruth. She

didn't sit home with an empty larder and complain about starving to death. She got out and worked.

Jesus considered work His norm. "I must work the works of Him that sent Me, while it is day: the night cometh, when no man can work" (John 9:4).

Paul repeated and enlarged the teachings. He told Christians to work with their hands. Then they would have enough for themselves and others, and wouldn't need to steal. (See 1 Thes. 4:11-12; 2 Thes. 3:10-13; Eph. 4:28; 6:5-9; Col. 3:17, 23-24.)

Ruth expressed her love for Naomi by work. What she did with her hands fleshed out the words she had uttered. In what ways do you express love with your hands? You express love as you earn money to support a household of loved ones. You express love as you cook a meal, or wash clothes, or make a bed. You express love as you build shelves in your basement, or mend a softball, or change a washer in a faucet. You express love as you can extra jars of relish for friends, or do some needlepoint for a loved one. How do *you* express love with *your* hands?

If we think of the story in a symbolic way, we could say that Ruth represents the great Gentile church. As we come to Christ, the "love of Christ constraineth" us (2 Cor. 5:14). We want to serve others. We express our love for Him by meeting the needs of others in practical ways.

How can we teach our children to work? The many sayings in the Book of Proverbs prove invaluable in teaching respect for work. Donald Grey Barnhouse, the great Bible expositor, had his children read one chapter of Proverbs every day. Thirty-one chapters in Proverbs, one for each day of the month. So they read it 12 times a year.

The Bible says work brings healthy rewards and satisfactions. As adults, we work all the time with some objective in mind. We work at some things as volunteers, to help others. We work at other things to make ourselves more comfortable. We work at still others for a paycheck. Or we work from a combination of these motives. Why do you work?

In teaching children to work we can systematically give rewards and satisfactions for tasks well done. One mother, sick in bed, couldn't persuade her teenage daughter to keep up with the laundry. All Sally needed to do was put loads of dirty clothes through the automatic washer and drier. But Sally procrastinated. The family was always running out of clothes. The parents decided to cut down on handing out money for high school needs. They offered to pay 25¢ a load for doing the wash. The laundry problem was solved. Said Sally, "I knew I had to do it, but I just couldn't make myself get at it when I should. The money helped."

I don't find anything in the Bible that says we must separate work from normal rewards. Paul even said the person who wouldn't work shouldn't eat (2 Thes. 3:10). God didn't rain bread from heaven into the laps of Ruth and Naomi. He gave them a chance to work. The bread He did rain from heaven for the Israelites had to be gathered. That meant work.

According to the Bible, the normal reward for work appears to be the privilege of eating. We shouldn't allow children to grow up with the idea that the world owes them food, shelter, clothing, an allowance, and a car without any responsibilities attached thereto. Given the opportunity, most children enjoy the self-respect of giving as well as receiving.

Next door to us live four little boys. The father gently coaches them in the joys of raking leaves, mowing grass, shoveling snow. The oldest, at only 10, has taken over their mowing and shoveling. He mows our lawn when we're gone. He considers the money he earns doing it fabulous. It helps get him to camp. I don't have any worries about what those boys will be like in their teens.

When our son Dan was 11, I was in bed for a few months. At that time I taught him to do the wash. It took three weeks of instructing, but he learned. Several years later he referred with pride to the time when he got his "job." He did the wash for a nickle or dime a load till he went away to college.

He and his brother and two sisters also earned half of their college expenses. They took enormous pride in those jobs of factory work, office work, delivering mail at Christmas. One worked as an orderly in a hospital, one as an elevator girl one summer. They learned to respect any kind of honest work. And ever after that, work seemed easy for all of them. My mother said, "Whatever you learn when young seems easy all your life." We rob our children if we don't teach them to work when young.

They're in the stage now, as young adults, of evaluating what their parents did. Like any parents, we made our mistakes. But they feel their work experience was good.

Ruth wouldn't have chosen gleaning as her life work. But she willingly did it as the only work available. An article in the *Wall Street Journal* says that in an era of 8,500,000 jobless in the country, 400,000 jobs go begging. Some of these jobs require skilled workers, like computer programmer, pipefitter, or shipyard welder. But other jobs go begging because unskilled workers may consider them too low in status or pay. If Ruth had considered the status value or expected income from gleaning, she would have declined the job.

Hans Selye, M.D., an authority on stress, says the Western world is racked by the unsatiable demand for less work, more pay. People view work as stress, and stress as something that wears them down, takes its toll. True, says Dr. Selye, stress is involved in many common diseases such as ulcers, high blood pressure, heart attacks, allergies, mental problems, even aging. But, he says, stress is the spice of life. People need work as they need air, food, sleep, social contacts, or sex. Successful activity, no matter how intense, he says, leaves practically no chemical scars in our bodies. It's unsuccessful work that causes stress and leaves the scars.

And Ruth found success in her work. Boaz' kind words gave her the feeling of self-respect she needed. Naomi's interest in her efforts increased Ruth's sense of achievement.

You and I can reduce the stress on our loved ones even if they must face hard jobs. We can express appreciation. We can give a sense of achievement at the end of a day's work.

"And she took it up and went into the city: and her mother-in-law saw what she had gleaned: and she brought forth, and gave to her that she had reserved after she was sufficed" (2:18).

Home from the harvest field. Home after the first day's work. How exciting to wait for the one coming home from a new job. What happened? Where did you work? How was your boss?

"And her mother-in-law said unto her, 'Where hast thou gleaned today? And where wroughtest thou? Blessed be he that did take knowledge of thee.' And she showed her mother-in-law with whom she had wrought, and said, 'The man's name with whom I wrought today is Boaz'" (2:19).

Ruth might have silently put the grain into jars for storage. She might have felt too tired to talk and resented the eager questions. But she didn't. She spread out for Naomi's amazement what she had gleaned. Then as further surprise, she brought out the parched grain from the noon meal.

What a beautiful picture of relationship. I used to love hearing about those jobs my children had. It seemed to me I was living six lives all at once. I loved hearing about life from the viewpoint of an elevator girl, or a factory worker, or an orderly. I could never in a lifetime do all those things myself. What a privilege to share in other people's doing of them. Ruth gave her mother-in-law the privilege of sharing in her experiences. She didn't hold back any information that might have interested Naomi.

Also, Naomi demonstrated the art of good listening. Who wants to talk if no one is listening? Naomi identified with Ruth. She didn't evidence jealousy of Ruth. She could have resented Ruth's experiencing all the excitement of the big wide world. She didn't remind Ruth that she herself had the first legal right to Boaz. Through identification, Ruth's triumphs became her triumphs.

How many people genuinely identify with you in your triumphs? Whom do you run to when something really good comes your way? How many people do you genuinely identify with in their triumphs? How many call you when something good comes to them?

Naomi genuinely enjoyed every detail as Ruth shared with her. They apparently made a habit of talking. Listen to your children when they're chattering to you about little things. If you do, they're more likely to tell you the big things.

As Naomi entered into the day's happenings, she immediately put events into perspective. She viewed with astonishment the large quantity of barley. No doubt she had found it hard to send Ruth out for such work. When Ruth came home enriched with presents, Naomi knew something beyond the ordinary had taken place. Ruth's lines had fallen in pleasant places (Ps. 16:6).

"And Naomi said unto her daughter-in-law, 'Blessed be he of the Lord, who hath not left off his kindness to the living and to the dead.' And Naomi said unto her, 'The man is near of kin unto us, one of our next kinsman'" (2:20).

Naomi recognized God's hands in Ruth's good fortune. Earlier, she had said that God had afflicted her bitterly (1:20-21). Now she revised her estimate and said He had not withdrawn His kindness to her and Ruth, or to those already dead.

The exciting part of Ruth's news of the day:

Boaz was one of their relatives through Elimelech. In fact, he was one who had the right to redeem. Did Naomi sniff romance in the air? We don't know. But we do know she felt profoundly grateful to God; Elimelech's kinsman had treated Ruth kindly that day. Naomi must have feared for the rude treatment Ruth could have received as a gleaner. Now, she rejoiced and prayed for God's blessing upon this relative of her husband, who was apparently assuming some responsibility for her and Ruth.

Laws and usages and degrees of responsibility differ by place and time. But the fact of kindred remains. Someone has said that we choose our friends, but God chooses our relatives for us. A youth director in our church counsels with many young people. He says numerous teenagers complain about their parents. He advises them, "Whatever their faults, these are the parents God has given you. They must be the ones He feels you need for your growth and training. Your challenge is to work out the best relationship with them that you possibly can."

Today people move about so much it proves difficult to maintain friendships. But family members can remain a constant point of reference in changing scenes. Though widely scattered, we can maintain relationships by letters, telephone calls, and visits. God has given us our relatives. I believe He wants us to take the trouble to maintain family ties. So many family connections pull apart for sheer lack of communication. It takes time to talk, but talking keeps relationships in repair. Your family may prove the only close grouping you can maintain for a lifetime.

In the Bible, relationships of family picture our relationship with God and with each other. God intends parents and children, brothers and sisters, to be close. The fact of relationship calls for consideration and regard. It may require overlooking hurts. It also at times may involve practical help. As we give it, we must always evaluate that help. What will be the longterm effect? Boaz gave very generously to Ruth and Naomi. But he gave in such a way as not to weaken them.

Did you notice Naomi's generous concern for Boaz? She wanted him to be especially blessed of the Lord for his liberality to them. A man less noble than Boaz might have ignored relatives in such straits. He could have preferred to forget the past, leave it buried, since Elimelech, the connecting link between them, had died.

"And Ruth the Moabitess said, 'He said unto me also, "Thou shalt keep fast by my young men, until they have ended all my harvest."' And Naomi said unto Ruth her daughter-in-law, 'It is good, my daughter, that thou go out with his maidens, that they meet thee not in any other field'" (2:21-22).

Ruth saw her work laid out before her. This was the time of harvest. She couldn't decide, "This morning I don't feel like working."

Today, the word *duty* has gone out of fashion. But a sense of duty helps in building relationships with other people. When impulse fails, duty can take over—like a reserve battery for charging an engine.

One spring and summer between college semesters, I worked for an insurance company. My job was to type a hundred bills a day. The job used up my eyesight and my capacity for sitting, so I couldn't read much. But I kept my soul alive by memorizing poetry as I rode to and from work. One of my favorite poems was Wordsworth's "Ode to Duty."

Stern Daughter of the Voice of God!
O Duty! if that name thou love
Who art a light to guide, a rod
To check the erring, and reprove;
Thou, who art victory and law
When empty terrors overawe;
From vain temptations dost set free;
And calm'st the weary strife of frail humanity!

Somehow that job, which I hated, did wonders for me. I discovered what work was. I discovered you could apply yourself for eight hours a day. My grades went up remarkably when I returned to school. Study didn't seem like work at all and never has since.

"So she kept fast by the maidens of Boaz to glean unto the end of barley harvest and of wheat harvest; and dwelt with her mother-in-law" (2:23).

Ruth pursued the opportunity that opened. She saw it as God's place for her. Our service as Christians is like Ruth's work in Boaz' field. We're to work in Christ's harvest field. He'll direct us. He'll tell us where to work—close to Him. The work may seem tiring and burdensome at times. The routine may pall. But close to Him, we find the little "handfuls of purpose," and His presence brightens the day, as Ruth's days in the harvest field were brightened by the smile, words, and touch of Boaz.

Are you working in the place of God's appointment? Check it with Scripture. With circumstances. With friends and people who love you. With the still small voice of the Holy Spirit speaking within you.

Ruth's tiring work opened out into an undreamed-of vista of opportunity.

7

When Should You Take Advice?

───────── ● ─────────

We all love to be asked for advice. How do you give it in such a way that people will seek your counsel? Most of us also need advice at times. When should you act on your own, and when should you ask for advice?

Ruth didn't ask Naomi for any advice in regard to Boaz. But Naomi saw the need and offered it. Ruth trusted her enough to accept.

"Then Naomi her mother-in-law said unto her, 'My daughter, shall I not seek rest for thee, that it may be well with thee?'" (3:1)

The last time Naomi said anything about rest— *menuchah*—was back in Moab. Ruth and Orpah were starting out with her for Israel. At that time she warned them not to come. She said she could promise them no *menuchah* in Israel. Orpah turned back. But Ruth came on, expecting no home or husband.

When it came to the hard job of going out to glean, Ruth made the proposal and Naomi acquiesced. Ruth concerned herself about Naomi's welfare. Now the thought for Ruth's welfare arose within Naomi.

When Naomi spoke of "rest," Ruth knew she was not referring to a holiday or vacation. She was referring to the rest you find in a home of your own. A place of repose for the affections. The position of unmarried women and young widows was perilous. The only place they could find safety and respect was in the house of a husband.

Naomi wanted Ruth to enjoy a sense of rest from her wanderings. A home would give her provision, freedom from the misery and temptations of poverty. Naomi wanted happiness for Ruth, the companionship of a good husband. She hoped to compensate her for the sorrows of her widowhood.

How generous of Naomi. She thought of Ruth's good regardless of where this would place her. She might easily have clung greedily to the twosome of herself and Ruth. She was willing to risk losing Ruth for Ruth's own good. Her unselfishness qualified her to offer advice.

Isn't giving up self-interest the secret to making husband, children, or friends to want our advice? Before presuming to advise, we must first put ourselves out of the picture. Look at things from the other person's point of view. You dare not advise selfishly.

Besides referring to a home, *menuchah* also meant fulfillment of a hope. That hope implied an end of trials and a change in fortune. Ruth had had enough changes in fortune to last a lifetime. We all like stimulation. We relish challenge and excitement. But too much change is harmful. We feel, "Oh that I had wings like a dove! for then would I fly away, and be at rest" (Ps. 55:6). But even flying away usually doesn't bring rest. The place of escape inevitably contains some flaw.

Ruth had already chosen the true rest that God offers. The Bible says the wicked can never find this rest, that they "are like the troubled sea, when it cannot rest" (Isa. 57:20).

God says we haven't entered into the Christian life until we attain a sense of rest in it. "There remaineth therefore a rest to the people of God" (Heb. 4:9). That rest starts now and lasts for eternity.

In addition to spiritual rest, Naomi now saw for Ruth the possibility of a home on this earth. Like any loving parent, she considered the possibilities for Ruth's good. The right kind of *menuchah* for Ruth would differ from the right kind for anyone else. We each have our own needs, our own kind of home or occupation.

Our word "rest" comes from an Anglo-Saxon term and like the Hebrew means either "repose" or "a resting place." It can last for eternity, for a lifetime, or only for a day or an hour. We need differing amounts of rest as well as differing kinds.

Land is given rest so it may produce more in coming years. We speak of the "heavenly rest," or of heaven as "home." A body must rest. A volcano can't spew forth lava indefinitely; it must rest. All nature must rest. John Ruskin, 19th-century art critic, once said, "There's no music in a 'rest,' . . . but there's the making of music in it. And people are always missing that part of the life melody."

The rest we find in our homes shouldn't become an end in itself. Rather, it constitutes a source of strength for going out to serve.

As each day of the harvest flew by, Ruth enjoyed more and more the presence of Boaz. She must have felt his eyes upon her, sensed his thought to be taken up with her. Even Naomi saw romance developing. Yet nothing happened. So Naomi came up with a plan.

" 'And now is not Boaz of our kindred, with whose maidens thou wast? Behold, he winnoweth barley tonight in the threshingfloor' " (3:2).

Three things stood in the way of marriage for Boaz and Ruth. First, Boaz was not the nearest of kin. Chapter 2 uses four different words in referring to the relationship of Boaz to Naomi. Verse 1 speaks of him as *moda,* "acquaintance or friend." Verse 2 uses *mishpachah,* "family." Verse 20 uses *garoph,* "near of kin," and a word of ultimate closeness in relationship, *goel.*

The second thing that stood in the way of marriage for Boaz and Ruth was Naomi herself. She held the prior right of marriage to the legal *goel.* Naomi could have claimed Boaz for herself. He knew this. As a God-fearing man, he would not have pushed her aside. How was Naomi to show she waived her legal claim in favor of Ruth?

The third thing that stood in the way of happiness for our lovers was Boaz' diffidence. He couldn't believe Ruth as a beautiful young woman would choose him, an older man. How was Ruth to indicate she preferred Boaz to the nearer kinsman?

If Ruth followed Naomi's plan, she would dissolve all these difficulties with one act. Not often does the mother of a girl's first husband help her find a second. This was the plan:

" 'Wash thyself therefore, and anoint thee, and put thy raiment upon thee, and get thee down to the floor: but make not thyself known unto the man, until he shall have done eating and drinking' " (3:3).

Certainly Naomi's plan was not out of harmony with customs of the day. Ruth wasn't claiming only a favor for herself. She was claiming a right for her dead husband and his family. Gleaners had to go to the landowner and claim their right to glean. Likewise a widow had to go to the *goel* and claim her right of marriage.

When Ruth first went out to glean, Naomi knew little about Boaz. By now, she had come considerably closer to him. Perhaps he had even called at their home, and conversed with Naomi. Certainly, as a far-traveled relative, Naomi would have much of interest to say. Or perhaps Naomi had heard from members of his household that tonight he would winnow on the threshing floor, located down the hill from town in a windy spot. He would winnow at night to take advantage of the evening breeze. Though a mighty man of wealth, he worked with his own hands.

We've already seen Boaz demonstrating good relationships with his workers. We've seen him carefully supervising processes of cutting, tying, and gleaning. Now he superintended the winnowing, even spending the night on his winnowing floor to protect his grain from robbers. As a conscientious businessman, he carefully guarded his property.

Boaz must have rejoiced at the good crop. Paul, preaching in Turkey centuries later, said God gives us a constant witness of Himself in the rain and fruitful seasons. He thereby fills our hearts with food and gladness (Acts 14:17). Every year God witnesses to us of His goodness (Ps. 65:11). However divorced we are from the simple life of Boaz and Ruth, we remind ourselves that every good and perfect gift comes from God (James 1:17). Boaz, out under the night sky, surrounded by his heaps of grain, would keenly have felt God's provision.

When Ruth gleaned, Boaz showered her with gifts. He went far beyond her legal claim on him. Naomi believed he would also go beyond his actual responsibility as distant relative. Yet the mission had to be carried out delicately. Naomi was interested in feelings. She wanted to make two people happy.

On the earlier mission, Ruth went out in working clothes. This time she was to deck herself in holiday attire. She risked humiliation that first time, because owners of land could say no to gleaners. This second mission involved risk also. The first time, she went asking for a few ears of grain. The second time she went to lay claim to Boaz' whole estate and person. She certainly risked humiliation if Boaz refused the responsibilities of *goel*.

Here the symbolism of Boaz as Christ becomes especially apt. Ruth risked all to place herself at Boaz' feet. She trusted his character, his love for her, his devotion to God. She believed he would not abuse her trust. She knew him well enough to believe he would not reject her.

Likewise, we take the risk of throwing ourselves at the feet of Jesus. Knowing Him, we are sure He will not take advantage of us, humiliate us, or reject us. We can safely place our lives at His disposal.

Throughout the ages, courtship has required cooperation from both man and woman. Every society has its little signals of willingness or unwillingness. My sister has been happily married for 30 years to a man she met on a train. He was a soldier on leave, traveling across the continent. Walking up and down the aisle, he looked for someone interesting to talk to. He sat down beside her. In the course of the conversation, she noticed a button had come off his coat. She whipped out a needle and thread and sewed it on.

On the way to his home in Maryland, he stopped over a day in Chicago. There he visited her at home. They kept in touch over half a continent for a few years while dating others. He found he couldn't forget her. He said sewing on that button strangely touched him.

In a former church of ours, a man who sang in the choir became a widower. An attractive woman 20 years younger than he also sang in the choir. One Sunday after evening service she invited him to her home for a cup of tea. He accepted, and two months later they were married. Said he, "I never dreamed she would be interested in me."

Naomi advised Ruth as to a signal that would say the word in her society. Naomi also knew something about human nature. The old cookbooks used to say, "The way to a man's heart is through his stomach." Naomi advised Ruth not only to wait till Boaz was through with the evening's work. She was also to wait till he had finished eating and drinking. Then she was to make her presence known.

Any sensible woman knows not to charge into her man's life just any old time. When he's busy with responsibilities, he can't give her his attention. But if she'll wait till he's relaxed, and alone, he's eager to turn to her.

In preparation for winnowing, animals threshed out the grain. Oxen would tramp round and round on it, till hulls came loose from kernels, and the straw was ground into chaff. Now in the fresh breeze men tossed up the threshed grain with winnowing forks. As the heavier grain fell directly into a pile, the breeze blew the chaff into another pile. After Boaz' helpers finished their work and their meal, they went home. Only Boaz as owner stayed.

W. M. Thomson, author of *The Land and the Book,* traveled in Palestine in the early part of this century. He found that scenes exactly like these in the Book of Ruth were common throughout the area. You can still see such scenes occasionally.

"'And it shall be, when he lieth down, that thou shalt mark the place where he shall lie, and thou shalt go in, and uncover his feet, and lay thee down; and he will tell thee what thou shalt do'" (3:4).

Naomi knew Boaz would lie down among the piles of grain. He would cover himself with his all-purpose cloak which served as a blanket by night. Ruth's uncovering his feet would symbolize her claim on him for marriage.

"And she [Ruth] *said unto her, 'All that thou sayest unto me I will do'"* (3:5).

Perhaps it all sounded rather daring to Ruth. But she trusted Naomi. She respected the older woman's knowledge of customs, as well as her sensitivity and common sense.

A good time for you and me to accept advice is when we come to the end of our own knowledge. Success, they say, is knowing your limitation as well as your abilities. Has someone earned your trust, as Naomi earned Ruth's? If so, you can risk moving beyond your own knowledge on another person's say-so.

Many times, friends and loved ones believe we can carry off something we don't feel qualified to do. Sometimes, the Holy Spirit in us tells us this or that is wrong for us. Then we have the right to refuse anyone's advice. But the Holy Spirit may say, "Go ahead, take the risk, you can't do any worse than fail. And if you do fail, you'll learn a valuable lesson by trying."

Check if you have the witness of the Spirit within you. See that the proposal checks out with Scripture. If so, then it's time to act on the advice of someone you love and trust. Take the risk— regardless of your own fears. Many times someone else can lead us out into undreamed-of avenues of possibility.

How would Ruth alone ever have surmounted all those barriers without Naomi's loving advice?

8

Social Convention—
Protection or Prison?

———•———

As we picture Ruth going down to the threshing floor to seek Boaz at night, we suffer culture shock.

"And she went down unto the floor, and did according to all that her mother-in-law bade her" (3:6).

Dressed in her finest, Ruth walked out at dusk through the gate of the town. She followed a trail curving downhill through olive groves, fig trees, and vineyards. Caves in the limestone hills sheltered farmers guarding crops through the night. She found Boaz, as expected, winnowing barley at his threshing floor. She stayed in the shadows till he had eaten and drunk and lain down to sleep.

"And when Boaz had eaten and drunk, and his heart was merry, he went to lie down at the end of the heap of corn: and she came softly, and uncovered his feet, and laid her down" (3:7).

The procedure sounds very strange to us. Even embarrassing. But I'd hate to have had my character judged by how I appeared to some French Canadians in Montreal.

Returning from Europe, one of our children developed a high fever and pain in her side. We took her straight from the ship to a hospital. The doctor diagnosed appendicitis, and operated that night. The next day Bart drove home with the other three children. I stayed in Montreal with Deborah.

But I could visit her only one hour a day. What should I do with the rest of the time? We'd been sight-seeing all around Europe. The obvious way to spend my time: explore Montreal.

Equipped with map and guidebook, I started out. But something was wrong. The first time I paused to study my map, a man approached me. He asked me to move in with him. I sat down on a park bench to rest a few minutes; a stranger invited me to his hotel for dinner.

I had always smugly believed that women who received such attentions did something to invite them. Why was I receiving such a rash of unwanted invitations?

Walking through a crowd one evening after dinner, I headed toward my hotel. Idly I scanned the faces around me. By chance, I caught the eye of a man in the crowd. Immediately he wheeled about and began following me. I only shook him by boarding a bus.

I got back to my room in a small hotel. Unnerved by my adventures, I went to bed at eight o'clock. The sound of a key turning in my lock wakened me. Then a hand reached in. I was terrified. My landlady explained in lightning French that she was only putting a letter on the dresser for me. She couldn't imagine anyone being in bed at that hour. I wanted terribly to go home.

Those attentions I received on the street strangely chilled me. I felt isolated from ordinary human contact. Why? I learned only the last day before Deborah and I flew home. In Montreal, at least at that time, women did not usually walk alone. I had walked all my life on the streets of Chicago, without feeling conspicuous. I simply didn't know the customs of Montreal. I had no idea of the signals I was innocently giving. Culture shock can prove very painful.

We shouldn't judge Ruth, or Naomi, by the signals Ruth's actions convey to us. They had entirely different meanings to Boaz.

The wind died down. Boaz completed his day's work, and ate his evening meal. The word translated "merry" in the King James version means literally "good." He felt at peace with the world, well-satisfied, relaxed. Ruth waited till he had fallen asleep. Then she crept among the piles of grain and uncovered his feet. There she lay down. We can imagine she didn't sleep. She just waited.

"And it came to pass at midnight, that the man was afraid, and turned himself: and behold a woman lay at his feet" (3:8).

We don't need to go to other cultures to find out what culture shock feels like. Alvin Toffler has written a whole book on the shocks of change we experience in our own time. He says the basic thing to get used to in our time is the fact of change.

So we ought to be able to adjust to the differences between our culture and Ruth's. As we find out what her actions meant to her and Boaz, we can understand them. The one thing sure about custom is that it changes. Customs at one time in the Bible are different from customs at another time.

To what extent should we follow conventions of the society around us? Some of us grew up on Emily Post. She laid out a correct way to do everything. Today her books seem strangely populated with servants. Who ever sees a servant these days? The whole approach to the architecture of houses and entertaining has changed. With the hostess in the kitchen, the counters and stove are open to the rest of the house. The hostess chats as she chops radishes or mushrooms. Emily Post is out of date. Conventions have changed.

Customs can be an enormous protection. The thing that made it perfectly respectable for a woman to walk about the streets of England or America alone was custom. No "gentleman" gave a second thought to a woman alone on the street.

Customs in many countries have protected young couples from some of the mistakes they make in our society today. Custom protected a boy from getting involved in responsibilities beyond his years. Custom protected a girl's virginity. A friend of mine lived in Spain for a while. She said "nice" families there never let their girls go out on a date alone with a boy. She must always have a chaperon, provided either by her family or the boy's. One girl's younger brother thought it great that his sister was dating so-and-so. He got to go to all the restaurants and other exciting places as chaperon.

But custom can become a prison. It must change with the times. Today, women are gaining new freedoms all the time. In *The Identity Society,* William Glasser says now it's even "correct" for a woman to initiate a relationship with a man who interests her. Such opportunities used to be— theoretically—reserved for that extra day of Leap Year. Now he says, she can invite him out to lunch, furnish her own transportation, and pay her own way. She can also decide whether or not she wants to invite him again. At one time if she didn't date she could only wait and wonder why men passed her by.

But when change comes too radically, people are driven out of safe grooves. They feel lost, without abiding values. Today, so many seemingly decent young men, with substantial homes and jobs, simply walk out on their families. They see someone else, and decide it would be more fun not to be married. With women's new freedom, perhaps they think they should have more freedom too. In church recently, I sat next to a beautiful young woman with her two boys. She told me she was going through a divorce. She never dreamed it would happen to her. But her husband was living with someone else. In another era, custom would have held him, if nothing else. Today, customs have changed so rapidly, people scarcely know where they fit in society.

In the simple agrarian society of Ruth's day, it took centuries for customs to change. Everybody knew where he belonged. Boaz knew exactly what Ruth was saying to him in uncovering his feet that night. When he roused at midnight, he was startled, but not shocked. He saw no impropriety in finding

Ruth at his feet. Other versions say simply
"startled," not "afraid," as in the King James version. The same word was used of Isaac—he
"trembled very exceedingly" at a dramatic moment
in his life. (Gen. 27:33) It was a dramatic moment
for Boaz. He wasn't in the habit of finding women
at his feet at night. Yet he respected the message
Ruth conveyed.

*"And he said, 'Who art thou?' And she answered,
'I am Ruth thine handmaid: spread therefore thy
skirt over thine handmaid; for thou art a near
kinsman'"* (3:9).

Here for "kinsman" Ruth used *goel*, one who had
the right to redeem. Boaz probably knew it was
Ruth before he asked. The romance had been
growing day by day. But he considered Ruth out
of reach. No passion is so potent as the one held
strongly in leash.

Ruth asked him to take the active step of putting his "wing" over her. The word translated
"skirt" is literally "wing" in the Hebrew. The
covering wing is a favorite symbol of protection
in the psalms and elsewhere. Translating that
metaphor into the language of action, the word
came to mean covering with the cloak. In the
wedding ceremony of that time, the groom put
part of his cloak over his bride's head. The act
symbolized his taking her under his protection as
wife. Among Bedouin peoples, even in this century, the wedding ceremony included covering the
bride with a special cloak. The groom would say,
"From now on, nobody but myself shall cover thee."

The skirt of the robe as the sheltering wing was

used of Jehovah, as the husband of Israel (Ezek. 16:8). Boaz one time said to Ruth that she had come to dwell under the feathers, the wing, of the Almighty. He meant she had trusted in God for protection, provision, and fellowship. Now he recognized that she was asking protection, provision, and fellowship of him as *goel*, or redeemer.

In an instant, Boaz understood all the implications of Ruth's act. She was asking Boaz to redeem her from her widowhood. He was to enter into her husband's inherited property, and to reinstate her dead husband's family in Israel. Her coming at night in this intimate way also showed one thing more—that she loved him as a person. Boaz trembled with excitement as he sensed his heart's desire lay within reach.

But as a man of character and principle, Boaz didn't seize her in that moment. Even though they were alone on the threshing floor, he understood the dignity of her message. He restrained himself from immediate pleasure to carry everything out decently and in good order. He realized Ruth was telling him that Naomi had set aside her claim. Naomi wanted Ruth to have Boaz, Boaz to have Ruth. And Boaz also knew that Ruth was telling him his age didn't matter.

"And he said, 'Blessed be thou of the Lord, my daughter: for thou hast showed more kindness in the latter end than at the beginning, inasmuch as thou followedst not young men, whether poor or rich'" (3:10).

Boaz commended Ruth for her high character. Perhaps he had seen young men attracted to Ruth.

Her ultimate kindness: to choose him over them. But kindness to whom? To himself, of course. But also to the memory of her husband. She might have looked only for sensual pleasure. If so, she would have chosen a young man. He saw her choice of himself as unselfish. Especially as a Moabite, Ruth might have ignored the responsibility of raising up progeny to her dead husband. Boaz referred to the kindness she had already shown to her mother-in-law as the "first kindness." She left her native land to follow and comfort Naomi. But he said this last kindness was greater even than that.

Apparently, Boaz had already thought through the whole responsibility of *goel*. He knew that as husband to Ruth, he would gladly perform all the responsibilities due Ruth's dead husband. He would also take care of Naomi. Ruth might have regarded the customs of Israel as a prison to which she couldn't adjust. Instead she accepted them, and they became to her a protection.

Boaz again called down God's blessing upon Ruth. And again, he answered his own prayer.

" 'And now, my daughter, fear not; I will do to thee all that thou requirest: for all the city of my people doth know that thou art a virtuous woman' " (3:11).

The word translated "city" means, literally, "gate." Everyone lived in the town, surrounded by its wall. Fields lay outside the town. Workers went out in the morning, came in at night. So the gate became an important gathering place for the whole city.

Ruth had made her way among a people strange to her. And customs, even small ones, can prove so painfully difficult. We stayed in Filipino homes, when we ministered there for a few months. At 4 A.M. we'd hear the clatter of pans in the kitchen. We'd know they were frying eggs. They wanted the eggs sufficiently "set" for us to eat at 7 A.M. And we discovered we might as well eat those eggs at 7 A.M. If we didn't, they'd show up again at noon, or again at the evening meal.

Out on the streets we'd hear vendors hawking something that sounded like "be-loot, be-loot," as men might hawk ice cream or hot dogs in our country. We learned that "be-loot" meant un-hatched duck embryos buried in the ground for six months or more to ripen. We didn't buy any.

In the mountains, among the Ifugao, our bus stopped for lunch. The meat offered looked like beef. On inquiring, we found it was dogmeat. That day we skipped lunch. Prejudice stopped our digestive juices.

But we found the Filipinos horrified at our custom of letting milk rot into cheese, or cabbage into sauerkraut. One woman said to me, "I don't know why Americans don't like our food. They eat that awful bloody meat. That seems barbaric to us. And they take off all the grease. That's what makes things good. We add grease."

Ruth had graciously accepted the customs of Israel, little and big. She came for the big reasons —to relate to a people who knew Jehovah. She didn't let the small things break her relationships. The town's suspicions of her had died as she accepted new customs appreciatively.

Boaz said everybody knew she was a virtuous

woman. And to get the picture of a virtuous woman in Old Testament times, we need only read Solomon's description of such a one (Prov. 31:10-31). The town now saw Ruth as a woman of strength, sweetness, ability. A woman who acted with determination, unselfishness, and resourcefulness.

The word here translated "virtuous" is that same word used of Boaz as a man of wealth, of Gideon as a mighty man of valor. It suggests force of both mind and character, general capacity. Maybe we should think of Ruth as a female "mighty man of valor." She certainly showed enormous bravery. "A virtuous woman is a crown to her husband: but she that maketh ashamed is as rottenness to his bones" (Prov. 12:4). Ruth was a match for Boaz. She would grace his home and his heart.

No doubt the town was impressed with Ruth's obedience to her mother-in-law. She showed self-discipline. They would also approve of Ruth's circumspect behavior toward young men. Any inconsistency would certainly prove obvious to all in that small town society. Her life was hidden from no one.

No doubt the townsfolk approved of the way Ruth accepted her poverty without complaint. They saw how hard she worked to improve her condition. She didn't talk about how strange the people of Bethlehem appeared to her. She didn't flaunt the special attentions Boaz showed to her as gleaner.

It has been said that a young man will treat his wife after marriage pretty much the way he treats his mother and sisters before marriage. Boaz saw Ruth treating even her mother-in-law well. He

knew she would show at least the same kindness
to a husband.

*" 'And now it is true that I am thy near kinsman:
howbeit there is a kinsman nearer than I. Tarry
this night, and it shall be in the morning, that if
he will perform unto thee the part of a kinsman,
well; let him do the kinsman's part: but if he will
not do the part of a kinsman to thee, as the Lord
liveth: lie down until the morning' "* (3:12-13).

Boaz possessed the kind of faith that expressed
itself in action. Even when offered the thing he
wanted most—Ruth—he thought of his responsibility. He considered the rights of Ruth, and the
rights of the nearer kinsman. Property was involved here, as well as marriage. He didn't want
to do any one else out of his rights. But with rights
go responsibilities. Society decays when people
look only at rights and forget responsibilities.

In public, Boaz acted with tender concern for
the well-being of Ruth. In private he also respected her rights. He assured her he would take
care of all her claims for her. She would not need
to approach the nearer kinsman herself. Boaz himself would assume that responsibility.

We all know of people who act one way in
public, another way in private. Boaz was not a
hypocrite. His behavior, even when no one was
looking, stood above reproach.

Perhaps Boaz knew already the other relative
would not act as *goel*. Still, he wanted to clear the
title to Ruth's property by approaching the man.

"And she lay at his feet until the morning: and

she rose up before one could know another. And he said, 'Let it not be known that a woman came into the floor' " (3:14).

Boaz and Ruth wanted each other terribly; yet they postponed consummation of their relationship till the proper time. The original Hebrew says she lay down at "the places of his feet." Somewhere in the area of the threshing floor. In these verses we see desire, and yet discipline. We sense the pulse of approach and appeal. Yet appreciation for God's order holds back appetite.

"Also he said, 'Bring the veil that thou hast upon thee, and hold it.' And when she held it, he measured six measures of barley, and laid it on her: and she went into the city" (3:15).

Boaz wanted Naomi to see some tangible evidence of his satisfaction with Ruth's offer. So he sent back a substantial gift. Six measures of barley was twice what Ruth had gleaned in a day. Yet it wasn't an overwhelming gift. He didn't want to raise Ruth's hopes too high at this stage of arrangements.

The gift would prove a heavy burden to carry as Ruth trudged up the hill. Yet she must have carried it happily as she went home to Naomi. Loaded with grain, she would look less questionable coming from the threshing floor at dawn.

Why six measures? Six throughout Scripture stands for labor and service. Six is followed by seven, the symbol of completeness, of rest. "Six days shalt thou labor. . . ." Whoever had served six years was released in the seventh. The six measures given to Ruth suggested that for Ruth the hard labor was over. Her day of rest, of *menuchah,* was at hand.

Ruth risked all to lie at Boaz' feet. Boaz kept his promises. He performed. When we put ourselves at Christ's feet, He likewise keeps His promises.

Ruth wanted first the person of Boaz. She loved him for himself. But he loaded her with gifts. Jesus says to us, "But seek ye first the kingdom of God, and His righteousness; and all these things shall be added unto you" (Matt. 6:33). Christ adds to the blessings of Himself good things to meet our needs.

9

God's
Part and Ours

———————●———————

What is God's part, and what is our part in providing for our needs? As a child during the Depression, one day I heard my father sputtering. That afternoon he had called in a home where the father was out of work. With his family fast running out of money, the man was sitting with hands folded. "The Lord will provide," he said.

My father trusted God, but he deplored such inactivity. He felt the man ought to be out looking for work, or making contacts. He ought even to be working for nothing, perhaps learning some new kind of work. Providing for a man's family struck my father as an inappropriate load to dump entirely on the Lord.

I've thought about the matter many times since. Many families, including our own, have been miraculously provided for in times of need. We've all heard marvelous tales of the Lord's provision. The people telling them sometimes are serving the Lord zealously; they let God take care of the wherewithal. Other times they're doing all they can for themselves; they quietly trust God for the rest. Does there ever come a right time just to sit still and wait?

"And when she came to her mother-in-law, she said, 'Who art thou, my daughter?' " (3:16)

Ruth returned from her crucial meeting with Boaz on the threshing floor. Her mother-in-law had waited with eagerness to learn how it all turned out. Did the plan work? Did Boaz rise to the bait of Ruth's offer of herself? Was she the betrothed of Boaz? Or was she still the poor widow of Mahlon? "Who art thou, my daughter?"

"And she told her all that the man had done to her" (3:16).

Ruth and Naomi openly communicated with each other. Naomi asked bluntly, not feeling any need for fussy caution in questioning Ruth. Ruth answered in detail. Naomi's attitude encouraged Ruth to talk freely. We see in their relationship a beautiful lack of jealousy. Naomi had long since given up any resentments in regard to Ruth. She might have felt some pain about another man marrying the wife of her dead son. She also might have suffered some pangs of jealousy for herself. After all, Naomi held first claim to the goel as husband.

Instead, Naomi entered into Ruth's joy, exulting in every detail. And Ruth told her all that had happened.

"And she said, 'These six measures of barley gave

he me; for he said to me, "Go not empty unto thy
mother-in-law"'" (3:17).

The seal of Ruth's venture was the grain she carried in her mantle, or veil. And he had even mentioned Naomi in connection with the gift, thus
giving tangible evidence to Naomi of his intentions.

Ruth's mention of "six measures" emphasized the
symbolic meaning of six. In the gift, both Ruth
and Naomi enjoyed a foretaste of fulfillment. More
was coming. Six comes short of perfection—seven.
We are still living under number six. But every
day the Lord gives us some little foretaste of the
coming glory of heaven. Or of the coming glory
of His reign on earth. One ancient writer says He
gives us daily "a little heaven to get to heaven by."
Ruth was coming to the end of her period of
anxiety and labor; she was soon to enter into her
time of rest in the household of Boaz.

"Then said she, 'Sit still, my daughter, until thou
know how the matter will fall'" (3:18).

In her listening, and in her responses to Ruth,
Naomi showed tender feeling. She also showed
genuine trust in God. Her words expressed common
sense—shrewdness and foresight, tact, and knowledge of human nature. Boaz had already experienced the dramatic disclosure of Ruth's feelings
for him. Ruth dared not do anything more, or he
would feel she was pushing him. And who doesn't
resent being pushed? All too often, pressure only
pushes a person the other way.

The other day a young woman called up in great
alarm. Her husband, very skittish about church

going, had been attending with her. Even enjoying it. He appeared to be growing spiritually to a remarkable degree. He even went along with his wife's desire to tithe their income.

Then a member called up to ask if the young couple would care to attend a series of membership classes. A pastor telephoned to arrange for a time to visit in their home. She didn't know how to say no. Yet the prospect of the call threw her husband into a tailspin. He interpreted the two phone calls as pressure.

At the last moment she got the message through. "Leave him to me," she said. "He's coming along. Just don't put any pressure on him." The young minister gladly cancelled the call, and the young man continued to grow—at his own pace.

Many a young man has skittered off into the wild blue yonder when a girl presses him for marriage. And sometimes a girl will discover innumerable flaws in a young man who starts pushing her for marriage.

Naomi was wise in regard to Ruth. When she saw something for Ruth to do, Naomi urged her to action. But she knew there was a time to wait, as well as to work. Now events must be left to others. In fact, to God.

The right time to sit still comes when we've done our part. A workman must first labor, then enjoy his weekend, or vacation. He puts in his day of toil, then enjoys his evening and night of rest.

The time to rest is when you've come to the end of your responsibility. Sometimes it's when you've come to the end of your ability. Waiting comes when you have done all you can. Trying to do more would only mess up the situation. Christ worked throughout His ministry. But there came a time when He stood silent before His enemies. He knew further words to be useless (Matt. 26:63).

Ruth was to wait, and yet she was a girl of action. She liked to make decisions, and follow them up with deeds. She had said to Naomi, "Whither thou goest, I will go." And she followed Naomi up that steep trail to Bethlehem. Ruth didn't spend time and energy in postmortems. She refrained from cutting open decisions of the past to see how other choices might have turned out. She pushed on with the travel and adjustments and hard work involved in her decision. She now had food in the pantry. The harvest was over. She had made herself acceptable to the townsfolk. She had declared herself to Boaz.

"Redeem our lost property," Ruth had asked of Boaz. Now she must leave her cause in her kinsman-redeemer's hands. In a similar way, you and I commit ourselves to Christ. Then we must learn how to wait for His good things to come to us.

How hard it is to wait. Have you circled above an airport waiting to land? So many planes are stacked up that it may take over an hour to land. In the meantime you miss your connecting flight. Should you burn up energy in frenzy, wishing that plane onto the ground? Or should you sit back, read, and conserve your strength? There are times when you can do nothing. You might as well compose yourself and wait patiently.

Ruth had done all she could. Naomi told her so. She must have felt tired after her days of work in the field and after her night of excitement. Now came her time to rest.

Sometimes people refuse to wait. They try to

take events into their own hands. God told Abraham time after time (Gen. 12, 13, 15—17) that He was going to give him numerous descendants. They would be as many as the stars and the sands of the seashore. Then God let Abraham reach age 86 with no sign of a child.

Sarah, his wife, became impatient with God's promising and not performing. She took events into her own hands. Sarah urged Abraham to follow the accepted custom of the time—have a child by Sarah's maid Hagar. So Abraham did. Ishmael was born—and became the father of the Arabs. The tension resulting from Abraham's refusal to wait still troubles the world. God let Abraham wait 13 years more before He gave him a child by Sarah. That child was Isaàc, later known as father of the Jews.

It's often hard to wait for a baby—sometimes years. But usually, you wait nine whole months. If you try to shorten the gestation period, the baby isn't fully developed. Often it's hard to wait for an embryonic babe to get ready to be born spiritually. It usually takes some months of prenatal development spiritually for that moment of rebirth to come.

While the Israelites camped in the wilderness, Moses went up on Mount Sinai to receive the Law. The people couldn't wait 40 days for him to come down. So they made a calf of gold, and worshiped it. God declared Himself ready to blot them out and start over again with Moses. We think they should have been able to wait 40 days, that "a God . . . who acts in behalf of the one who *waits* for Him" deserved a people willing to wait (Isa. 64:4, NASB).

After Israel was settled in the Promised Land, they encountered more trouble about waiting. When enemies threatened, they were always wanting to turn to human agencies for help. In Isaiah 30, God pronounced woe upon the pro-Egypt party— those who wanted to turn to Egypt for help. At that time God sent word through Isaiah, "Their strength is to sit still" (30:7).

Sometimes our strength is to sit still; yet we spoil things by grabbing for human help. Perhaps an illness is the kind that simply won't yield to drastic measures. The doctor urges "conservative" means of treating it. A change of diet. A lifelong change in life-style. More rest. But no. We go to him demanding an operation, a strong drug, action. It's up to him to get us well. Many people have pushed doctors into bad decisions just by refusing to sit still and wait.

God said a lot of good things in Isaiah 30 as He tried to persuade those Israelites to wait. "In returning and rest shall ye be saved; in quietness and in confidence shall be your strength: and ye would not" (30:15). You can insist on turning to human agencies, like horses and fighting men. But if you do, you'll simply be routed by swifter horses and stronger fighting men. Or you can stop and simply wait for the Lord to act. Doing nothing, you'll come out ahead. In fact, he says, God is even then waiting to be gracious to those who wait for Him (30:18).

Imagine. God is just holding back the blessing He wants us to have. He's waiting for us to give up our schemes. He wants us to look to Him alone —after we've done the sensible things He expects us to do for ourselves. He didn't give Boaz to Ruth right away. He waited until she had worked hard the whole season in the harvest fields.

Thomas, disappointed and heartsick after the crucifixion of Jesus, couldn't wait with the disciples. He disbelieved the promises of God and of Jesus Himself. So Thomas went off by himself. He missed the wonderful experience of Resurrection Day.

But some people, like Ruth, do know how to wait. The disciples in the upper room knew how to wait. Jesus told them they were not to leave Jerusalem until the coming of the Holy Spirit "not many days hence."

God had given these disciples many appearances of Christ, many infallible proofs. But they had to wait 10 whole days with no more proofs. How did they manage it? They gathered together with others of like faith. They spent the time in prayer, getting ready to carry on the work of Christ. So they were all with one accord in one place. Then the Holy Spirit came on the Day of Pentecost.

"'For the man will not be in rest, until he have finished the thing this day'" (3:18).

Naomi knew Boaz as a man of responsibility and integrity. He would carry out his promises. She also knew him as a man of action who wouldn't procrastinate. He wouldn't putter over details of the day while he postponed this matter of crucial importance. Businessmen sometimes find themselves making telephone calls or shuffling papers to postpone an important decision or interview. A minister can fill up his time with meetings to dodge hard study or calling. A housewife can postpone tackling the big job of the day by dallying at little jobs. Boaz, like Ruth, was a person who acted promptly on his decisions. That fact alone boded well for their congeniality in marriage.

Boaz had begun a good work in providing for Ruth. Naomi expressed complete confidence that he would continue it. God who has begun a good work in us will not quit until He has performed it (Phil. 1:6). Sometimes, we get tired of waiting for God to do something in someone else's life. But God has promised. Sometimes, we need to sit down and reread some of God's promises. Naomi reminded Ruth of Boaz' promises. Sometimes the very exercise of waiting teaches us things we need to learn.

"The Lord is good unto them that wait for Him, to the soul that seeketh Him. It is good that a man should both hope and quietly wait for the salvation of the Lord. It is good for a man that he bear the yoke in his youth" (Lam. 3:25-27). Ruth had born the yoke of widowhood and hard work. These disciplines prepared her for the discipline of waiting.

You have to learn how to wait. Two months after I was married, my husband had to go to another city for a week. I felt desolated—I didn't yet have any program of my own. So I left my small apartment to visit my mother. She gave me scant sympathy. "Just see how much you can get done while he's gone," she advised.

Look at waiting as a time of opportunity. Fill up the empty time with things that need doing. Paul honed the art of waiting to a fine edge. You remember that sermon he preached in Athens, on Mars Hill. Paul hadn't marked out Athens as a center for any major strategy. He was just waiting for Silas and Timothy to catch up with him from Berea. They planned to proceed to Corinth, where he would stay for 18 months. But did Paul just sit in Athens, anxiously waiting for Silas and Timothy? Not Paul. His spirit got stirred up by the idolatry he saw. He spent every day arguing with Jews in the synagogue. He also reasoned with devout persons, and with the general public in the marketplace. He accomplished all that—while just waiting. Paul might have said, "I have no plans for Athens; I'll not do anything until we start our real work in Corinth."

Ruth had the promises of Boaz to go on. We have the promises of God and of Christ to keep us through the waiting times. Sometimes, we wait for death through a dread disease. Sometimes we wait for prayers to be answered. Sometimes, when God has a special lesson to teach, He waits for things to get really bad before He answers. Sometimes we have to wait for results from an examination, or from some paper we've written. Sometimes we wait anxiously for the return of a loved one.

God has promised us many rewards for waiting. He says if we just wait on Him, He'll exchange our weariness for His strength. We'll mount up with wings like eagles. He'll give us power to do the impossible. He promises we'll run and not be weary. He'll help us to organize, and set priorities. He'll guard us from crashing into obstacles. He also promises He'll enable us to walk when the going gets rough. He'll then keep us from fainting. He'll give strength to put one foot in front of the other when we think we'd rather lie down and die. All that comes from waiting on Him (Isa. 40:31).

David gave us a great psalm on waiting. He had

had to wait long years after God promised him the kingship. He knew about waiting while Saul chased him around the country trying to kill him. Even after Saul died, David had to wait seven years for the people to come to him as king. David communed with God, and came to terms with waiting.

Here's David's advice: don't spend your time fretting because evildoers seem to be getting what you want (Ps. 37). God will take care of them. "Delight thyself also in the Lord; and He shall give thee the desires of thine heart" (vv. 3-4). Don't get impatient. "Commit thy way unto the Lord; trust also in Him; and He shall bring it to pass" (v. 5). What will He bring to pass? The desires of your heart. If you're fully in tune with God, you'll only want what He wants for you. If you'll wait for Him, He'll give it to you. "Rest in the Lord, and wait patiently for Him" (v. 7). "Wait on the Lord, and keep His way, and He shall exalt thee to inherit the land . . ." (v. 34).

God lays out for us a time to work, and a time to wait. Sometimes, our work consists of waiting. When the English poet John Milton went blind, he figured out that sometimes you serve God by waiting.

When I consider how my light is spent
Ere half my days in this dark world and wide,
And that one talent, which is death to hide,
Lodged with me useless, though my soul more bent
To serve therewith my Maker, and present
My true account, lest He returning chide:
"Doth God exact day-labor, light denied?"
I fondly ask. But Patience, to prevent
That murmur, soon replies, "God doth not need

Either man's work or his own gifts; who best
Bear His mild yoke, they serve Him best; His state
Is kingly: thousands at His bidding speed,
And post o'er land and ocean without rest;
They also serve who only stand and wait.

10

What Does the Law Require?

Two people had fallen in love. No lack of money stood in their way. Ruth had none, but Boaz possessed plenty. No difficulties of health blocked their union. Both demonstrated good physical condition as they worked long hours in the harvest fields.

No obstacle of intellectual difference kept Ruth and Boaz apart. They had enjoyed ample opportunity to talk as they ate together. They often brushed against each other in the work of the day. No difference of religion made marriage inadvisable. Ruth had thrown over the pagan gods of Moab to worship the living God of Israel. Boaz recognized immediately that Ruth shared his warm devotion to Jehovah.

Both had experienced life. We don't know what griefs or losses were in Boaz' past, but most people who reach his years have tasted trouble. Ruth, though still young, had suffered enough for one much older. They could understand each other in depth. Mature love contains its own unique joys.

What obstacles yet lay in the way of love's consummation? Only technical ones. The law said a Moabite couldn't enter into the congregation of the Lord even to the tenth generation (Deut. 23:3). Even an Edomite or an Egyptian could enter in the third generation. The law of the *goel* provided for Ruth as wife of a deceased Israelite. But could that law overleap such an obstacle as Moabitish origin? The whole problem of the plot turned on this point. Was there any way of surmounting the law?

"Then went Boaz up to the gate, and sat him down there" (4:1).

Remember, Boaz had spent the night on the threshing floor, far below Bethlehem. He climbed the hill to reach town, and stopped at the gate even before going home.

The gate in the East served many uses. It often corresponded to the forum or marketplace in the West. People met there to sell or barter their produce. The gate served as senate hall or parliament house. People looked to the gate as a place of primitive justice. Town elders gathered at the gate to discuss news of the day. Anyone who wanted to could stand around and listen. Some squatted, in oriental style. The gate constituted the place of morning and evening lounge.

Boaz could expect that eventually his kinsman would either go out through the gate to his fields, or come in from his threshing floor. The gate, a short tunnel, offered shade and breezes. Stones or stone benches afforded seats for some. People moved at a leisurely pace, no one rushed or pushed to make a precise appointment. They simply waited.

Boaz acted according to Naomi's knowledge of his character. He didn't draw out the proceedings unfeelingly from day to day. He might have even put off definite action from week to week, month to month. Or even year to year, as some do with long attachments. "Hope deferred maketh the heart sick" (Prov. 13:12).

Do we sometimes keep people waiting unnecessarily? Someone has said, "A gift quickly given is twice given."

Boaz stands as a model of promptitude. He acted quickly. Of course, his promptness tells us how involved his own emotions were. He felt as eager as Ruth to bring the matter to a conclusion. Think of what his promptness said to Ruth.

A man from Austria was talking to me about his adjustments to American life. He said he found great difficulty getting used to Americans' carelessness with promises. In Austria, as in America, people sometimes said, "I must have you over to my house." But in Austria you would expect an invitation within the week. Here, it might come months later, perhaps never.

How do you feel about an invitation or a gift long promised, long deferred? Doesn't it shrink in value as time goes on?

Ruth could conclude she stood at the top of Boaz's priority list. He cared. He showed that he cared by carrying out his promise immediately. Sometimes we hurt a child keenly by promising lightly without following through right away.

Yet a very real obstacle stood in the way of marriage for Boaz and Ruth. However much Boaz esteemed and prized her, he loved and honored the law of God more. He would risk losing his heart's desire to honor that law.

"And behold, the kinsman of whom Boaz spake came by; unto whom he said, 'Ho, such a one! Turn aside, sit down here.' And he turned aside, and sat down" (4:1).

We see here the whole course of an ancient legal procedure. By sitting at the gate, Boaz plainly declared he sought a judicial proceeding. When the person he sought came by, he addressed him with a formal summons. The one addressed seated himself without delay, as requested. No doubt he knew of the matter of Naomi's property. He knew sooner or later he would have to face his responsibility.

Before the police and court system developed, kinsmen protected the rights of wronged relatives. Boaz had already been referred to (2:20) as "one of our next kinsman." The word *goel*, meaning redeemer, is often translated "kinsman" because the kinsman acted as a redeemer. *Goel* means literally "one who unlooses."

In Korea, kinship obligations remain very strong. A young man in that country got into financial difficulties. He would have gone to prison if he couldn't come up with some money. His parents-in-law made their living by a small-loan business. They turned over their entire principal, $60,000, to rescue their son-in-law from disgrace. Then they had to find another way to make a living.

Many individuals in this country also feel a strong sense of family responsibility. A young farmer in Illinois mortgaged his land to borrow $40,000. This he invested in a single herd of choice beef cattle. He planned to fatten them for market, sell at a good profit. But the price went down. He nearly lost the farm his parents had left him. His brother and sister each put in $5,000 to save his inheritance of land.

Time and time again in the Bible, the word *redeemer* applies to Jehovah. Many times He intervened in history to rescue Israel from captivity. Job in his wretchedness maintained a sublime faith that God would rescue him. Said he, "For I know that my Redeemer—*goel*—liveth, and that He shall stand at the latter day upon the earth" (Job 19:25).

Redeemer is used repeatedly of Christ. He paid the ransom for us. He set us free from the bonds of evil desires that make slaves of us. He set us free from the power with which Satan seeks to entrap us. All this symbolism of Christ as Redeemer is based on the Old Testament idea of *goel*. So it is important for us to understand just who the *goel* was. Exactly what was he responsible for?

The Old Testament *goel* bore three obligations.

He was to avenge a brother's murder. No police organization existed. Only the avenger gave pause to one angry enough to kill (Num. 35, Deut. 19, Josh. 20). Satan is out to destroy us. Christ alone can stand up to him. " 'Vengeance is mine, I will repay,' saith the Lord" (Rom. 12:19). Whatever damage we suffer, we don't need to take judgment into our own hands. Our Kinsman-Redeemer Christ can take care of anyone who has wronged us.

The *goel* was to buy back his brother's property if poverty compelled him to sell it. Property was to stay in the family, generation after generation.

Thus God provided for broad land distribution. He didn't want land all gravitating into the hands of a few as it has in many countries (Lev. 25:25-27).

The *goel* was to buy back his brother's freedom. Sometimes a man had to sell himself into slavery to pay his debts. If so, his *goel* was the one to free him by paying off those debts (Lev. 25:47-55). Christ paid off the debt for all of us who have sinned and come short of the glory of God. We are bought with a price (1 Cor. 7:23). We can't pay our own debt to free ourselves. "No man can ransom himself or give to God the price of his life" (Ps. 49:7, RSV).

The *goel* carried responsibility to raise up a successor to his brother. Sometimes, a brother died leaving a widow but no offspring. If so, the brother or nearest male relative was under obligation to marry the widow. The first son born would count as the dead brother's issue (Deut. 25:5-10). To the Jews, no branch of the family tree was to perish. What was broken off by death was to be grafted back by the *goel*. Christ as *goel* restores us to man's original relationship with God.

As bridegroom, the *goel* represents another figure of speech used of Christ. He took to Himself His bride, the church. Ruth, as Boaz' bride, a Gentile, represents the church which today is largely Gentile (Rom. 11:13-31). In company with Christ, the church produces spiritual offspring. Without Him, the church suffers the barrenness of widowhood.

So the *goel's* task was to loose that which was bound. He brought a captive back to his home. He bought a slave for freedom. He released a piece of land to its rightful owner. He restored a widow to her family position.

We see many parallels, and some differences between Boaz and Christ as redeemers. Boaz went out from his house. Christ went out from His home in heaven. Boaz went to the gate, Christ to earth to redeem. Both redeemed in the presence of all the people, Boaz at the gate, Christ at Calvary. Paul said of Christ's redemption, "This thing was not done in a corner" (Acts 26:26).

Boaz' redemption was recognized at the time. Christ's was not. Boaz was honored. Christ was not.

Both Boaz and Christ redeemed in the manner prescribed. Each knew the right thing to do, and did it in the right way. Boaz followed the well-known marriage rules for the *goel*. Christ followed the ancient law of the universe—"without shedding of blood there is no remission" of sin (Heb. 9:22).

Serving as *goel* involved the right, the will, and the power to act.

This whole legal ceremony with the unnamed kinsman established Boaz' *right* as next nearest of kin. God the Son became our nearest of kin by taking on Himself our flesh. Christ, our elder brother, is qualified to redeem us (Heb. 2:9-18). He said all of us who do the will of His Father in heaven are His brother, and sister, and mother (Matt. 12:50).

A near relative had to demonstrate the *will* to redeem. He didn't become *goel* automatically. Said Boaz, "I *will* do the part of a kinsman to thee." The nearer relative of Elimelech's had not stepped forward to demonstrate his will be redeem.

In the case of the blood-avenger, the *goel* enjoyed no choice. But in the case of marrying a widow, only a moral obligation existed. Boaz was willing because he loved Ruth. The Lord Jesus is willing because He loves us.

A *goel* also had to possess the *power* to redeem. No amount of willingness or right relationship could fully qualify him. Sometimes a willing and rightful redeemer didn't have enough money to act. He couldn't buy back the person or property of his brother, however much he might want to. He might not even be able to afford the expense of tracking down a slayer. A would-be *goel* might lack sufficient means to marry his brother's wife and support her.

Boaz possessed the means. He owned broad fields below Bethlehem. Christ possesses all the riches of glory with which to redeem and support us (Phil. 4:19).

Some friends of ours went through great difficulties with their son. He got into trouble with the law for selling stolen automobile parts. When police broke the ring he was part of, the news hit the headlines. The parents thereby learned the "ring" had its headquarters in their garage. They had supposed the boys who hung around were just a bunch of their son's friends.

The parents, with police help, took the boy to a mental hospital. Psychiatrists found nothing wrong with him—only a "character defect." The boy left home and got into more trouble. His grieving parents lost touch with him. One night the telephone jangled them out of sleep. "This is the city jail. Your son is here." They got out of bed, went to the jail. They posted a huge bond to get him out.

The judge released him to their home. Their act of posting bond for him touched the young man deeply. At last, he felt all the grief he had caused them. Chastened, he couldn't do enough for his parents. He washed walls, did housework, gardened. Eventually, someone gave him a job.

Today this son is an upstanding citizen, leader in his church, father of a family. His parents acted as *goel*. They had the relationship, the willingness, and the power—the financial resources—to redeem him.

Who acts as *goel* in your family? Each of us has the opportunity and the obligation from time to time. We know we should rescue a loved one in trouble. We can ask God for willingness and resources to act in redemption.

"And he took 10 men of the elders of the city, and said, 'Sit ye down here.' And they sat down" (4:2).

A crowd of ordinary citizens assembled about the two relatives, Boaz and the unnamed kinsman. But the 10 elders formed the necessary official witness.

"And he said unto the kinsman, 'Naomi, that is come again out of the country of Moab, selleth a parcel of land, which was our brother Elimelech's' " (4:3).

Naomi considered herself too old to become a wife (1:12). Yet her property could not go to any blood relative without marriage. As long as she lived, her husband's name remained upon his property. She held the same right and power to dispose of it that the law gave to him.

Actually, the land itself never could be ceded. What Naomi was selling was only temporary rights to crops until the year of Jubilee. This came every 50 years. At that time all property reverted to its original owner. Again we see God's concern for broad land distribution. Large estates of land have cursed many countries throughout history. They have reduced multitudes to serfdom or slavery. "But they shall sit every man under his vine and under his fig tree" (Micah 4:4). Thus the Lord describes the ideal conditions of the millennial age.

" 'And I thought to advertise thee, saying, "Buy it before the inhabitants, and before the elders of my people." If thou wilt redeem it, redeem it. But if thou wilt not redeem it, then tell me, that I may know: for there is none to redeem it beside thee; and I am after thee' " (4:4).

Boaz offered the land to the unnamed kinsman—honestly and wholeheartedly. Yet his heart must have told him just to buy it for himself.

Many times today two lovers want to possess each other immediately. They don't want to wait to get circumstances all in order for marriage. They won't wait till families have become reconciled, everyone satisfied. Yet, in rushing too fast to physical union, they miss some of the finest fruits of love. They miss bringing their entire personalities and all their relationships to the union. Boaz risked loss to make everything right before God and before society.

"And he said, 'I will redeem it' " (4:4).

The closer relative seemed to acquiesce. Was Boaz to lose what he so earnestly desired? The unnamed relative would be glad to get the property. And the widow went with the property.

But no. Boaz moved smoothly on. He had really set things up rather cleverly. He didn't have the lovely Ruth present. The sight of her might soften the man's heart. He didn't have Naomi there to press her case. Sometimes a *goel* refused a widow's direct request. She then had the right to pull off his shoe, and spit in his face. He would ever after be known as the one who had his shoe pulled off (Deut. 25:5-10). He would thereby suffer disgrace for refusing his responsibility as *goel*. Boaz made refusal as easy as possible.

"Then said Boaz, 'What day thou buyest the field of the hand of Naomi, thou must buy it also of Ruth the Moabitess, the wife of the dead, to raise up the name of the dead upon his inheritance'" (4:5).

Notice how Boaz threw in the term "Moabitess." He knew that would discourage the kinsman. Boaz reminded him likewise about the law of inheritance. He must support Ruth as wife. Yet her first son would inherit her property in the name of her dead husband, Mahlon.

"And the kinsman said, 'I cannot redeem it for myself, lest I mar mine own inheritance; redeem thou my right to thyself; for I cannot redeem it'" (4:6).

The deal was off. The unnamed kinsman, representing law, could make no exception in favor of Ruth, a Moabitess. The law excluded her. All of us are excluded by the law (Gal. 3:10-11). All of us have failed to measure up in one way or another. Only

Christ can make an exception of us. He loves us as Boaz loved Ruth. As Boaz recognized her heart's trust in Jehovah, so Christ recognizes our heart's trust in him. Love covers up for a multitude of imperfections.

The unnamed kinsman stood rigid. He had no feeling toward Ruth. Perhaps he feared the same fate as came to Elimelech, Mahlon, and Chilion and didn't want to risk such a marriage. Since Ruth was a Moabitess, he declined what he would otherwise consider an absolute duty. By so doing, he became another nameless Bible character who forfeited a place of honor in the lineage of King David.

The upshot: Boaz gained Ruth. The way stood clear for them to marry. Boaz risked losing what he most wanted to bring his actions in line with God's law. God gave to him what he longed for.

The unnamed kinsman, representing the law, was afraid. But true love knows no fear. "Perfect love casteth out fear" (1 John 4:18). Love—grace —can go beyond law. Christ went beyond the law and fulfilled the law. He redeemed us that we might become His bride.

11

Love's Fulfillment

"The closing will be on Friday, at 11:00 A.M.," the real estate agent told Bart. "You and your wife are to be there with a cashier's or certified check for the seller's equity in the house. The seller will be present with the title insurance policy and a warranty deed."

Living in a house of our own looked very inviting to us. Both of us had grown up and lived all our lives in houses owned by the church. A "closing" represented a new experience. It involved papers, signatures, and a transfer of property.

Boaz carried out a closing on some property in Israel. That closing involved a shoe—a sandal, such as people wore every day.

"Now this was the custom in former times in Israel concerning the redemption and the exchange of land to confirm any matter: a man removed his sandal and gave it to another; and this was the manner of attestation in Israel" (4:7, NASB).

The ceremony of the shoe had become extinct by the time the Book of Ruth was written. Yet that ceremony replaced a still earlier custom. Then, they set the foot on the land as a symbol of possession.

What did a shoe mean to the ancient Israelite? The shoe symbolized motion and wandering. God told the Israelites to eat the Passover feast in readiness to leave Egypt promptly. They were to have shoes on their feet, and staff in hand (Ex. 12:11). Eating with shoes on the feet implied extreme haste. It would be like our eating with hats and coats on. (See Ezek. 24:17, 23.)

The shoe also symbolized rest and possession. With the shoe one trod the earth. Hence, on holy ground, it must be pulled off. Anyone who visits mosques in the Middle East today knows he must remove his shoes. Sometimes, those stone floors or courtyards feel mighty chilly underfoot. You see masses of shoes and people at the entrance. Sometimes you wonder if you'll ever see your precious shoes again. But leave them you must if you wish to enter.

At the burning bush, God told Moses, "Put off thy shoes from off thy feet, for the place whereon thou standest is holy ground" (Ex. 3:5).

The captain of the Lord's host told Joshua, at Jericho, "Loose thy shoe from off thy foot; for the place whereon thou standest is holy" (Josh. 5:15). People removed shoes at mealtimes, in every sacred place, in presence of sacred persons. They took off their shoes on an occasion of mourning.

A person held complete control over his shoe. Therefore it symbolized the power of the possessor over his possession. Taking off the shoe on holy ground meant admitting God's possession. God expressed His possession of Edom—"over Edom will I cast out my shoe" (Ps. 60:8; 108:9). A man could tread on his possession with his shoe, any time, at his own pleasure. If he entered into possession with another person, he put his foot into the same shoe.

We talk about filling another person's shoes. A son timetimes suffers in trying to fill his father's shoes. It's not easy. One can understand why a kinsman might want to refuse acting as *goel*.

"So the closest relative said to Boaz, 'Buy it for yourself.' And he removed his sandal" (4:8, NASB).

Thereby, the kinsman said he gave up all right to walk on Naomi's land as owner. He surrendered to Boaz all claims to right of possession when he handed over his shoe. Doing this voluntarily, he suffered no degradation, as when the widow pulled off the shoe.

"And Boaz said unto the elders, and unto all the people, 'Ye are witnesses this day, that I have bought all that was Elimelech's, and all that was Chilion's and Mahlon's, of the hand of Naomi'" (4:9).

The transaction stood complete. Signed, sealed, and witnessed.

"'Moreover Ruth the Moabitess, the wife of Mahlon, have I purchased to be my wife, to raise up the name of the dead upon his inheritance, that the name of the dead be not cut off from among his brethren, and from the gate of his place: ye are witnesses this day'" (4:10).

Boaz stated his concern for redeeming Mahlon's family. Perhaps he remembered Elimelech, Mahlon, and Chilion with affection. He was aware of his own place in the family tree. He considered it important to keep all its branches intact. His love for Ruth prompted him to marry her, of course. In addition he enjoyed the warm glow of keeping all relationships alive.

We all owe much to the dead. We recall dead teachers who formed us. We remember spiritual leaders who inspired us. We remember friends who warmed us. Great people of history influenced us.

My mother has been dead for 20 years. Yet sometimes, when my rings click on the dishes as I cook or clean up, the sound reminds me of her rings clicking on the dishes. I cook much the way she did. In church, with certain hymns we sing, I feel I'm sitting beside her. When I teach Bible classes, I feel her approval. When disasters come my way, I keep putting one foot in front of the other the way she did. Psychologists call this "internalizing." In what ways are your parents' characteristics and feelings internalized in you?

David, like all the rest of us, owed much to his ancestors. He had internalized the value of honoring the dead. After long miseries, David at last became established as king. He immediately searched out someone left of the house of Saul. He learned of the crippled Mephibosheth, son of Jonathan, grandson of Saul. David gave to Mephibosheth all that was Saul's. He also insisted that Mephibosheth eat at the king's table, with David's own sons. All this David did for love of Jonathan, now dead.

Somehow it satisfies our emotions to honor the

dead. It seems to bring wholeness or completeness to our lives. Within reasonable limits, we should honor their wishes. You can't cut the dead out of your life without feeling cut off at the roots. If your past gives you only bad memories, you can turn it over to God. You can also work through those memories, step by step. But you can't ignore the dead, whether they helped or hurt you.

Boaz wanted wholeness or completeness in his life. He wanted to do the right thing by Mahlon and Elimelech. Whatever mistakes they had made, he wanted to redeem the family. He loved Ruth for herself. But his carrying out of the *goel* transaction surrounded their union with feelings of wholeness. People everywhere share the feeling that kindness to those left behind by the dead represents kindness to the dead themselves.

One little girl of a family of four suffered from "brain fever" at age two. She became deaf, and seriously retarded. She could perform simple tasks, but needed the protection of a home. Her parents kept her in their home till they died. Then a sister took over. When that sister died, another sister took responsibility for the handicapped one. These sisters did it out of love for their parents.

Boaz took upon himself a joyous task in marrying Ruth. But he risked all the losses the unnamed kinsman feared. He accepted large responsibilities. He took on Naomi as well as Ruth. He promised to bring up a child for his dead kinsman.

"And all the people that were in the gate, and the elders, said, 'We are witnesses'" (4:11).

Boaz carried out all arrangements for marriage decently and in order. Publicly. He sought no liaison with Ruth. He didn't even try to marry her secretly. Full-orbed marriage consists of commitments made: (1) to God, (2) to each other, and (3) to society. Neglect of any one means less than complete marriage. Boaz wanted all three.

He had said to the elders and all the people, "Ye are witnesses this day" (4:9). And they responded, "We are witnesses."

A witness is one who has seen what happened. He chanced to be on hand to view an accident, or a crime. Boaz' witnesses stood about voluntarily to watch proceedings. A witness not only has seen certain things, but is willing to admit he's seen them. Sometimes people refuse to step forward as witnesses to an accident or crime. They don't want to get involved. They play the part of the cowards.

Jesus said to His disciples after the last supper, as He was about to leave them: "And ye also shall bear witness, because ye have been with Me from the beginning" (John 15:27). He never told us we were to argue for Him, or fight for Him. He told us to witness for Him—simply tell what we ourselves have experienced. We thereby get involved.

"The Lord make the woman that is come into thine house like Rachel and like Leah, which two did build the house of Israel: and do thou worthily in Ephratah, and be famous in Bethlehem'" (4:11).

All the people wished Boaz well. Ruth had won her way. They knew her as loving and virtuous, and as a very hard worker. Now they wished her well too. The greatest blessing for an Israelite woman was to bear many children. Rachel bore only two, but her husband loved her dearly. Leah bore six sons and one daughter. Both women became ancestors of the nation. The Bethlehem townsfolk wished for Ruth the blessings of both Rachel and Leah. Even though she was a Moabitess, they hoped for her all that came to these Israelite women.

We're told to "Rejoice with them that do rejoice, and weep with them that weep" (Rom. 12:15). Sometimes weeping with people in sorrow proves easier than rejoicing in others' good fortune. Yet good wishes form a necessary part of all relationships. We need to take time for the congratulatory call or note. Most people experience enough trouble in their lives. With kind wishes we can help each other savor the good moments.

"*'And let thy house be like the house of Pharez, whom Tamar bare unto Judah, of the seed which the Lord shall give thee of this young woman'*" (4:12).

Why Pharez? First, because Pharez, son of Judah, was an ancestor of Boaz. Judah, one of the twelve sons of Jacob, headed the tribe in which Boaz appeared.

A second reason for mentioning Pharez is that his family seems to have been particularly numerous. His father's tribe was the largest at the time of the numbering. Pharez' two sons' families were mentioned as the important ones in that tribe (Num. 26:19-22).

A third reason for mentioning Pharez is that his mother, like Ruth, invoked the law of the *goel* to bring about his birth. Here the similarity between Pharez' mother, Tamar, and Ruth ends.

Ruth invoked the law of the *goel* delicately, in an aura of true love. Tamar invoked it as a legal right, without any pretense of love. When the law failed to secure her her rights, she resorted to trickery (Gen. 38).

Tamar, Pharez' mother, married Er, the son of Judah. He "was wicked in the sight of the Lord, and the Lord slew him" (38:7). Judah commanded his second son, Onan, to raise up an heir for Er by Tamar. Onan pretended to, but actually cheated; the Lord slew him also (38:10).

So Judah told Tamar to wait in her father's house until Judah's third son, Shelah, would grow up. Then she should become Shelah's wife, and raise up a son to Er. But Tamar saw that when Shelah grew up, she was not given to him as wife. Therefore she took things into her own hands.

Since Judah's wife was now dead, Tamar suspected she would find him open to a proposition. He went away from home for sheep-shearing, a festive time. She disguised herself as a prostitute along the way. She enticed him, then asked for her price. He offered a kid from the flock. As a pledge till he would send it, she asked for his signet, bracelets, and staff. When he came back with the kid, she had disappeared.

Later it came to Judah's ears that his daughter-in-law had played the harlot; she was pregnant. His judgment on her: "Bring her forth, and let her be burnt" (38:24). She produced his signet, bracelets, and staff, and proclaimed him the father.

Then Judah admitted she'd been more righteous than he. He had failed to give her to his son Shelah. "And he knew her again no more" (v. 26).

A strange story? Of course. It's injected in the

midst of the inspiring story of Joseph. Why? Some say it shows how much the Israelites needed to get out of Canaan at that time. Their moral standards had become hideously tainted by the local inhabitants. In Egypt they'd be off by themselves, in a separate portion of the land. There they could grow into a nation more truly representing God's moral standards.

Yet the child of this tarnished union between Judah and Tamar became an ancestor of the mighty Boaz. Even an ancestor of Christ. We see how God can rule, and overrule. We see how God uses the "weak things of the world to confound the . . . mighty" (1 Cor. 1:27).

Perhaps the very crudeness of Tamar's use of the custom of *goel* acts as a foil. It enhances by contrast the lovely story of Ruth and her *goel*, Boaz.

12

Love's Reward

―――――――― ● ――――――――

A young woman enjoyed travel. She felt sure a baby would not interfere with extended trips to Europe. She would simply leave the baby with someone. After a difficult pregnancy and birth, she produced a baby. Then she found she couldn't bear the thought of leaving that baby for any lengthy period. She didn't return to Europe for 15 years. Then she took all four children with her. What happened to her jaunty idea of walking off from her baby? Through the pain of childbirth, she became a mother. I know; I was that young woman.

Many aspects of growth and suffering go into the making of a mother. Ruth grew into motherhood through the discipline of delay, the discipline of sorrow, the discipline of determination, and the discipline of work.

"So Boaz took Ruth, and she was his wife: and when he went in unto her, the Lord gave her conception, and she bare a son" (4:13).

Ruth's first marriage produced no child. She failed then to attain the dream of every woman of her day. She learned patience through the discipline of delay. She lavished on husband and mother-in-law the love she might have given a child.

Other women in Scripture didn't wait as patiently as Ruth for a child. Sarah urged her husband to impregnate her handmaid, Hagar. Sarah couldn't wait for God to fulfill His promises to Abraham through herself. She brought untold suffering on herself and others by her impatience (Gen. 16-18, 21).

Hannah became very impatient with not having a baby. She sulked and complained at her husband, Elkanah. Said he, "Hannah, why weepest thou? and why eatest thou not? and why is thy heart grieved? am not I better to thee than 10 sons?" (1 Sam. 1:8) Poor Elkanah. He loved Hannah, but could not give her what she wanted.

Elisabeth, mother of John the Baptist, waited like Ruth. In an exemplary way. She grew old, past the time of childbearing. Yet Scripture records of her and her husband, Zacharias, "And they were both righteous before God, walking in all the commandments and ordinances of the Lord blameless" (Luke 1:6). Elisabeth devoted her thought to pleasing God, rather than to grieving, rebelling, or complaining.

In growing up, girls and boys, too, need to learn patience in postponement. We dare not try to grant their every wish instantly. If we do, we rob our children of opportunities for growth. Sooner or later they will want things we can't give them—like a husband or a certain job. We all need to learn how to cope with frustration.

Ruth prepared for motherhood through the discipline of sorrow. A scale of relative stresses puts losing a spouse at the very top of the list. Somewhere below that comes a jail term, personal injury or illness, being fired from the job. (The "Social Readjustment Rating Scale" was prepared by psychiatrists Thomas H. Holmes and Richard Rahe.) Ruth suffered other stresses that appear on this list. She changed to a different line of work. She suffered all the changes that go with moving to a new country.

By faith in God, Ruth stayed serene and trusting through all this. Readiness for motherhood means training for suffering. The pain of childbirth represents only the beginning. A mother suffers with every bump and fall of the little one. She suffers through his sicknesses and disappointments. She suffers when her children leave home. Thereafter, she suffers with all the difficulties that come their way. Trusting God means learning to handle occasional periods of stress.

Ruth prepared for motherhood through the discipline of determination. She learned to make decisions and stay with them. She didn't expect to be babied because she gave up much in coming to Bethlehem. Ruth already had demonstrated she could follow through on decisions. She stuck by Naomi through poverty. God expects Christians to live up to vows of marriage. He also expects them to live up to vows taken at a child's baptism or dedication.

Ruth prepared for motherhood as she learned the discipline of work. Most of us need to hold a job or two in the process of growing up. We thereby gain a conception of sticking to a responsibility. Caring for a child means meeting his needs. You don't search your feelings to find out whether you feel like cooking a meal or cleaning up a mess. You do it.

Ruth knew the discipline of love. A child does not know how to love automatically. He must learn to love. Ruth would be well-qualified to teach the art of loving. Her love had reached across chasms of difficulty. She knew love as an abiding commitment. Ruth loved her first husband, and her mother-in-law. Now she loved her second husband and her child.

In this arrival of a child, we see compensation for Naomi and for Ruth. They had suffered graciously. Now we see their unselfishness rewarded. We see Boaz fulfilling his own prayer (2:12) of blessing for Ruth.

"And the women said unto Naomi, 'Blessed be the Lord, which hath not left thee this day without a kinsman, that his name may be famous in Israel'" (4:14).

The kinsman-redeemer for Naomi, referred to here, is not Boaz. It is the baby, Obed. He counted as Naomi's own grandchild. Notice that these closing verses of the book focus on Naomi. The book started with her.

What a contrast between Naomi's earlier condition, and that now. When she returned to Bethlehem the women had eyed her with cold curiosity. Now they gathered about her with warm good wishes. Adversity had vanished. Ruth was no longer the poor gleaner but the happy wife of Boaz.

Naomi was radiant with some of the finest joys

of old age. Her daughter-in-law had become a mother, she a grandparent. Rejoicing neighbors surrounded her. Naomi considered Ruth's happiness more important than her own. Now Ruth became the means of Naomi's prosperity. She would know comfort and joy in her declining years.

All rejoiced over little Obed. Ruth would have rejoiced that an heir would carry on Mahlon's name. Naomi would rejoice that Elimelech's family line had been revived. Boaz would think of Elimelech, Mahlon, and Chilion, and be glad that their names would not be cut off from among their brethren.

Ruth would also rejoice for Boaz' sake, because of the child that would brighten their home. She would rejoice for Naomi's sake, who now possessed a line of descent. Boaz would rejoice over the joy and consolation of Ruth and Naomi. Naomi would rejoice that God was no longer dealing with her bitterly (1:20). Love and delight shined back and forth from person to person and grew brighter by reflection.

"'And he shall be unto thee a restorer of thy life, and a nourisher of thine old age: for thy daughter-in-law, which loveth thee, which is better to thee than seven sons, hath born him'" (4:15).

Naomi's bereavements left her with not much—just a foreign daughter-in-law. Ruth couldn't make up to her for all she'd lost. Still Naomi didn't spurn Ruth. She treasured Ruth for herself.

A present-day young husband walked out on his wife and child. The wife went home to her parents. They did everything they could for her. But feeling bitter toward her husband, she showed no appreciation to her parents. It's all too easy for us to destroy all of our other relationships when one fails us.

Naomi had made the most of what she had. Now the neighbors said this one daughter-in-law was worth more than seven sons to Naomi. The number *seven* in Scripture represents completion, perfection. The neighbors meant Naomi could have asked for nothing more than she had in Ruth. Even an Israelite blood relationship—sons—would have fallen short compared to the heart relationship with the Moabitess.

Jesus puts the heart relationship first. Love transcends all law, creates new relationships.

"And Naomi took the child, and laid it in her bosom, and became nurse unto it" (4:16).

Ruth trusted Naomi to take care of her son. Again, we see Ruth's generosity. She didn't require total possession of her child. She could share him with Naomi.

Do you share your children with grandparents? Grandparents can enormously enrich the life of a child. They offer love, and special insights. They can teach skills, they can help in holding up values. The child gains a sense of belonging to a larger family than that of father and mother. In some countries, grandparents assume the major responsibility for rearing children.

Good grandmothering involves its own responsibilities. It's easy for a grandmother to develop favorites. She may prefer the quiet child to the lively and heedless one. Love will keep her from showing favoritism. She must avoid developing a pique against one child.

A good grandmother won't undermine parents' discipline. They're the ones who have to live with the child, day in and day out. She'll ask before she bestows a gift or a treat. She won't try to buy the child's affection. She won't try to steal his heart by softening discipline.

A good grandmother won't be too busy to enjoy a relationship with each grandchild. A woman who holds a responsible position as an administrative assistant devotes one week a year to her five grandchildren. She drives East, picks them up at their homes. For one week the five little cousins enjoy her home and swimming pool in Michigan. Then she and her husband drive them back.

Naomi, as nurse, enjoyed the privilege of shaping little Obed. She lost the children of her own body. Now she boasted a son in the spirit of true love. She could form Obed in the pattern of Israelitish life and culture, and instruct him in the Law of God.

Because Ruth loved Naomi so much, little Obed would reflect her love. Mothers sometimes poison their children against father or grandparents. Mothers can also foster an attitude of love—both subtly, and openly.

"And the women her neighbors gave it a name, saying, 'There is a son born to Naomi'; and they called his name Obed: he is the father of Jesse, the father of David" (4:17).

No doubt the child's parents gave him a name, probably one that belonged to the family. But the name given by the women continued as his usual name. The name *Obed* means servant, or serving. Perhaps they saw in the little tot certain qualities of helpfulness.

Quite often we see distinctive qualities in very small children. A little girl of 11 months lay in her playpen studying a piece of cellophane. She crinkled it, turned it about, scrutinized it from every angle. She stuck with it for an hour and a half. Said her grandmother, watching through a glass door, "That child is going to be a student." In time the girl earned a Ph.D. degree with relative ease. Holding herself to the discipline of study was easy for her.

Others early show strong inclinations to neatness, sociability, athletic prowess, finger dexterity —or the opposite. We need to let each child be himself. Perhaps those names people gave children in biblical times helped them to become distinctively themselves.

Little Obed must have endeared himself to all as he wanted to do things for people. Not only his relationships, but his nature made him a nourisher of Naomi's old age. Serving represents the highest ideal for a Christian. Jesus took upon Himself "the form of a servant" (Phil. 2:5-8). "Let him who is the greatest among you become as . . . the servant" (Luke 22:26, NASB).

"Now these are the generations of Pharez: Pharez begat Hezron, and Hezron begat Ram, and Ram begat Amminadab, and Amminadab begat Nashon, and Nashon begat Salmon, and Salmon begat Boaz,

*and Boaz begat Obed, and Obed begat Jesse, and
Jesse begat David"* (4:18-22).

When David ruled as king, stories that came down
through his family suddenly became important.
People wanted to know his ancestry. The story of
Ruth gave some background for the character of
David.

Yet humanly speaking, Israelites would not have
felt this story reflected well on David. It showed
Gentile blood in his veins. But God wanted us to
have this story. He wanted to show us the greater
importance of faith over blue-blooded ancestry.

This story of Ruth introduces us to David. It
gives background for certain incidents and attitudes in his life. David apparently was aware of
his Moabitish ancestry. When in trouble with
Saul, David asked protection for his father and
mother from the king of Moab. They stayed with
the king of Moab as long as David was in distress
(1 Sam. 22:3-4).

In spiritual perception, the Book of Ruth stands
at the doorway to the Gospel. It demonstrates
God's openness to people of a country other than
Israel, and shows the kindness of God's gracious
plans for those whom He chooses, and who choose
to follow Him.

The family line in these verses is repeated in
Matthew's genealogy of Christ (Matt. 1:3-6). The
Moabitish ancestry of Ruth became part of the
human ancestry of our Lord. Ruth was one of only
four women mentioned in the genealogy of Christ.
Of these, Tamar gave birth through an illicit relationship with her father-in-law. Rahab made her
living as a harlot. Bathsheba conceived out of

wedlock. Ruth alone was unstained in character, but she came of Gentile blood. The Book of Ruth takes us back to our spiritual roots, and reminds us that God's ways are always high and creative, and graciously full of love.

The story of Ruth looks not so much to David as to Christ. Those included in the ancestry of Christ give hope to us all. By faith you can find your own distinctive place in God's scheme of things. By faith you can establish that most important relationship of all—with God through Christ. From this one, all other relationships draw their quality and strength.